Karen Leigh Davis

American Shorthair Cats

Everything about
Purchase, Care,
Nutrition, Health Care,
Behavior, and Showing

Filled with Full-color Photographs

Illustrations by
Michele Ea

BARRON'S

2 CONTENTS

A HISTORY OF THE AMERICAN SHORTHAIR

Domestication of the Cat

Most experts agree that the modern domestic cat, *Felis catus,* probably descends from an African wildcat called *Felis lybica.* This short-haired, feral feline resembles its modern-day relative in size and in tabby-striped coloring. While today's American Shorthair comes in more than 80 different colors and patterns, many representatives of the breed still retain the distinctive tabby markings and the lithe, muscular body of this wild ancestor. In fact, according to registration totals, the two most common American Shorthair colors are the silver tabby, which sports black stripes against a silver background, and the brown tabby, which has black markings on a reddish brown background.

History generally credits the Egyptians with being among the first people to domesticate the cat approximately 3,500 to 5,000 years ago. Astute agriculturists, the Egyptians most certainly recognized the cat's inestimable value in protecting their grain stores from rats and mice. One might imagine that the Egyptians began enticing prowling wild felines to stay close to their settle-

Enthusiasts changed the breed's name from Domestic Shorthair to American Shorthair to distinguish the breed from nonpedigreed lookalikes.

ments, perhaps by leaving scraps of food near their grain stores. As a result, taming or *domestication* of wild cats gradually took place. So valuable was their natural pest-control service that cats enjoyed an extended period of elevated status during this early era of human civilization. In fact, archaeological discoveries suggest that Egyptians worshipped cats as household gods, mourned their loss when one died and even mummified their remains for entry into the afterlife.

Arrival in the New World

Domestic shorthaired cats probably arrived in the New World with European immigrants aboard sailing ships in the 1600s. The breed lore even mentions the *Mayflower* as a possible mode of transport. Although difficult to prove, this tale is not implausible, since cats were brought along on long sea voyages in those days to hunt the rats and mice that ate the ship's food supplies. Owing to this practice, today's American Shorthairs most likely are descendants of those cats brought from the British Isles and other western European countries.

Upon arrival in the New World, the cats were released and likely extended their pest-control duties in and around the new colonies being settled. For centuries, these working cats flourished in the fields and barns of America's pioneers, allowing natural selection to mold them into a durable and dependable breed.

Not until the early 1900s, however, did serious cat enthusiasts begin to selectively breed these cats to preserve their mild temperament and natural hardiness. Interest was spurred, perhaps, as a result of the introduction of foreign cat breeds in the early twentieth century that began to dilute the naturally pure bloodlines of the domestic shorthairs flourishing on native soil.

As cat shows and the *cat fancy*—the collective term used to described those interested in breeding and showing purebred cats—began to develop in America, common barn cats began to be held in low regard, compared with the more exotic breeds available abroad. Many of these imported longhairs and Siamese cats were allowed to run free, and as a result, kittens began to crop up with varying coat lengths, color patterns, and temperaments. People who admired the domestic shorthaired stock realized they would have to mount an organized effort to retain the cat's original fine qualities.

The All-American Cat

Ironically, the first American Shorthair to be registered in the United States was imported from Great Britain. He was a red tabby male named Belle of Bradford. The breed originally was called simply the Shorthair, then later changed to the Domestic Shorthair. Over time, however, domestic shorthair became a term used to describe any shorthaired cat, until finally it became synonymous with even the mixed or random-bred cat. To eliminate some of this confusion, the name American Shorthair was adopted in 1966. The move was essentially a successful public relations effort that aimed to better represent the breed as the All-American Cat. Enthusiasts also credit the name change with helping people recognize that the American Shorthair is a distinct breed of shorthaired cat.

While it's certainly possible that a nonpedigreed or random-bred shorthaired cat that you see roaming today's North American streets and neighborhoods may resemble a purebred American Shorthair, the true test is in whether an animal can consistently produce kittens of the same conformation, coat quality, and temperament. American Shorthairs typically have round heads and full-cheeked faces with sweet, open expressions. Viewed in profile, the forehead and nose are joined by a gently concave curve, instead of the straighter, more pointed nose seen in common street cats. The body is solidly built, powerful, and muscular. The easy-care coat is glossy and mink-textured. Achieving this consistency in appearance and type is the fundamental purpose behind selective breeding and recording the many generations of cats in particular bloodlines.

Consistently ranking in the top ten most popular breeds of cat, the American Shorthair is truly one of the most beloved and attractive pets in the United States. The breed is also enormously popular in Japan. Today, the breed ranks as the eighth most popular out of 36 recognized breeds, based on the Cat Fanciers' Association's 1997 registration totals. It is also the sixth most popular shorthaired breed, according to the registration totals, with the Siamese and the Abyssinian holding the top two positions, respectively.

Association Recognition

The American Shorthair was among the first five breeds to be recognized by the world's largest registry of purebred cats, the Cat Fanciers' Association (CFA), when that organization was founded in 1906. Besides the CFA, there are numerous cat registering associations currently active in North America. (For a list, see page 92.) The American Shorthair is recognized for championship status—which means it can compete in the champion classes and earn titles—in all of these associations.

These associations not only register cats, they also verify the pedigrees and set rules for breeding and showing. The pedigree of a purebred cat lists several generations of its recorded ancestors. In addition to maintaining stud books, the associations sanction shows, present awards, charter clubs, train judges, and approve breed standards.

Practices regarding the acceptance of a new breed or a new variety of an existing breed, vary from one cat-registering association to another. In general, a new breed must meet certain criteria before it achieves recognition. Typically, a specified number of the cats have to be registered and shown for a period of time under what's called *provisional* status before the breed becomes eligible for scoring awards and points in championship competition. Depending on the association, the provisional class may be called the New Breed and Color, or NBC, class or category.

Personality Traits

Easygoing: The breed's hallmark is its loving, easygoing temperament. Because of their gentle nature, American Shorthairs make excellent pets, according to breeders. They also have a reputation for being highly amiable around children, dogs, and other pets.

Playful: A gentle, easygoing temperament doesn't mean these cats aren't playful. Quite the contrary; they are active, but not overly so. Because their bodies are muscular and athletic, they need opportunities for play and exercise to stay in shape and to keep from getting fat, so when you invest in an American Shorthair, you would be wise also to invest in several cat toys and a carpeted cat tree to encourage climbing and playing. Better still, why not get two cats, so they can romp and play with each other? You'll have an opportunity to compare and savor each feline's unique personality while they enjoy each other's companionship.

Intelligent: Having developed as a product of natural selection on the American frontier, the American Shorthair is a hardy breed whose survival depended largely on well-honed predatory skills combined with a keen, instinctual intelligence. These cats are determined problem solvers and seem to prefer toys that challenge them to chase or hunt down their imaginary prey. Being people-oriented, they also enjoy interactive play with their owners.

Loyal and affectionate: American Shorthairs thrive on human companionship and are well known for developing steadfast, devoted attachments to their owners. Not all of them are lap cats, but they are loyal and loving. They tend to select one individual in the household as their favorite person whom they will sit beside or follow from room to room. Ever curious, they like to be right in the middle of things and prefer spending their time in the rooms where you spend your time.

ACQUIRING YOUR AMERICAN SHORTHAIR

Before You Buy

Many people who are considering a cat as a pet question whether they should adopt from a shelter or buy a pedigreed animal. The choice is a matter of personal preference. Of course, acquiring *two* cats can be the perfect solution to this dilemma, if your lifestyle and financial situation permit. American Shorthairs have a reputation for getting along well with other pets in the household, so why not buy one purebred cat and adopt a second companion from your local animal shelter? Like people, cats can become bored and lonely when forced to stay alone all day while you are away at work. One way to avoid this is to get two kittens so they can bond as friends and keep each other company. Besides, owning two cats is twice the fun.

Mixed or random-bred cats make just as good companions as purebred felines, and they are much less expensive to acquire; however, purchasing a purebred cat has some special advantages. Most important, a purebred cat has a recorded ancestry, which means that certain health factors and other qualities, such as temperament and appearance, are more predictable. These inherited qualities, enhanced by genera-

The American Shorthair silver classic tabby sports black stripes against a silver background.

tions of selective breeding, are what you pay for when you buy a pedigreed cat.

If your ultimate goal is to show cats, then you'll eventually want a purebred to compete in championship classes; however, most major cat shows also have a special household pet category for exhibiting unpedigreed, random-bred cats. Many cats exhibited in this category were rescued or adopted from shelters. And many seasoned cat show exhibitors got their start showing in this category, learning the rules along the way. In household pet classes, cats are judged according to their beauty, condition, and personality rather than the breed standard. (For more information on cat shows, see Showing Your American Shorthair, page 89.)

Whether you decide on a purebred or a mixed breed, or both, remember that your relationship with any new cat could last a decade or longer. Because American Shorthairs tend to be long-lived with good nutrition and veterinary care, your purebred pet may give you an average 15 to 20 years of companionship. Are you prepared to care for a cat that long? For greatest compatibility, the cat you select as your long-term companion should suit your personality and lifestyle. Before you commit, know what you want in a cat. For example, do you prefer a male or a female cat? Do you want an adult cat or a kitten? Finally, are you looking for a cat to show, or do you just want a nice pet?

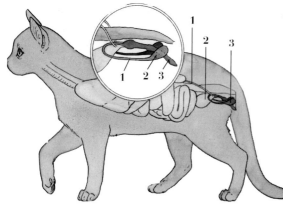

1. vas deferens; 2. testicles; 3. penis.

The following information may help make these decisions easier.

Male or Female?

Sex should not make a difference, unless you intend to become a breeder. If you simply want a pet, both male and female American Shorthairs make equally fine companions when altered. If you have no interest in raising litter after litter of kittens, you should alter your cat when it reaches the appropriate age. You can still show your American Shorthair in premiereship or alter classes after it has been spayed or neutered.

The telltale signs of whether a kitten is a male or a female are, of course, under the tail. In the female, the genital opening looks like a small slit and appears directly below the anus. In the male, the anus and penis are spaced farther apart, and both openings are round.

Veterinarians traditionally recommend that males be neutered between eight and ten months old and that females be spayed at six months. The surgery can also be performed earlier. In fact, to

Neutering a male cat makes him unable to reproduce and reduces or eliminates undesirable spraying behaviors.

ensure that indiscriminate breeding does not happen, some breeders elect to spay or neuter their pet-quality kittens early, *before* they sell them. This practice is becoming much more accepted, as studies have shown that early spaying and neutering appears to be safe and does not adversely affect feline maturity, as was once thought.

Generally, early spaying takes place between 12 and 14 weeks, and early neutering is performed between 10 and 12 weeks.

Spaying a female cat costs more, because the operation involves opening the abdomen to remove the ovaries, tubes, and uterus. Neutering the male cat is a less invasive procedure that involves removing the testicles. Remember, however, that the one-time cost of spaying a female is still considerably less than the long-term cost of raising and finding homes for successive litters of kittens. If cost concerns you, ask your breeder, veterinarian, or local animal shelter about low-cost spaying and neutering programs available in your area.

Benefits of spaying or neutering: Both operations reduce an animal's natural desire to leave the relative safety of its territory and search for a suitable mate. Eliminating this biological urge makes the animal a much nicer pet and improves its chances of living a longer, healthier life. Animals allowed outside to roam in search of mates are more likely to be killed by cars, injured in fights, or exposed to contagious diseases. Repeated veterinary bills for treating cats injured while roaming and fighting can quickly exceed the one-time cost of spaying or neutering.

Spaying eliminates the female's bothersome heat periods along with her ability to become pregnant. The operation also eliminates the possibility of any disease or infections in the organs removed and decreases the chance that breast cancer will occur later in life.

Neutering the male reduces aggressive behaviors, eliminates testicular diseases, and decreases the chance of prostate cancer later in life as well as diseases in other glands affected by male hormones. Neutering also helps curb a male cat's tendency to spray urine in the house to mark his territory.

Contrary to popular myth, your American Shorthair will not grow fat and lazy after being spayed or neutered unless you consistently overfeed it. As in people, obesity in cats is primarily caused by too much food and too little exercise.

Controlling pet overpopulation: Another reason to spay or neuter your American Shorthair is to help control the pet population surplus. About 75 percent of cats taken into U.S. shelters are euthanized (humanely put to death) each year, simply because there aren't enough homes to go around. Annual humane death figures have fluctuated from a staggering 4.3 million to nearly 9.5 million since 1985. Countless other homeless cats fall victim to neglect, starvation, and other hazards of life in the wild. Responsible cat owners and breeders make it their moral duty to alter pets and to prevent indiscriminate breeding by not allowing intact cats to roam freely.

On being a breeder: Breeding purebred American Shorthair cats should be undertaken by only the most serious and dedicated cat fancier. It is an expensive and labor-intensive hobby. Stud fees can range from $500 to $750, depending on the male's quality, color, and show record. If the stud is a grand champion or a national winner, you can count on the fee being even higher. Figure in the travel costs of transporting the female cat to the stud for breeding, the veterinary bills, vaccinations, cat food, advertising expenses, and so forth, and you can quickly see how little one profits from raising a litter of kittens.

Even after writing off allowable expenses on their business taxes, most professional breeders consider themselves lucky if they break even. To them, the real profits in breeding are intangible achievements, such as a Best in Show rosette, regional and national awards, and the respect of fellow cat fanciers who recognize their contributions to the American Shorthair breed. If these aspirations do not interest you, leave breeding to the professionals, and have your pet American Shorthair spayed or neutered.

Spaying is an operation that removes a female cat's ovaries, tubes, and uterus so that she cannot have kittens.

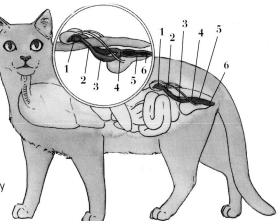

1. ovaries; 2. fallopian tube; 3. uterine body; 4. cervix; 5. vagina; 6. vulva.

Before acquiring an American Shorthair, make sure your children and other family members are not allergic to cats.

Many people have the notion that breeding their cat just once will allow their children to witness the miracle of birth. Unfortunately, this notion only adds to the pet overpopulation problem, even if you take the time to find the kittens good homes, so, instead of breeding your cat, teach your kids how important it is for all of us to take responsibility for the animals already in this world. Teach them how proper health care, spaying, and neutering can reduce the suffering that more than eight million surplus and homeless pets endure each year. Concentrate on being the best-educated pet owner you can be, and share your knowledge with others. Read books about cats. Subscribe to cat

magazines. Volunteer at your local animal shelter. Set an example as a responsible cat owner.

Adult Cat or Kitten?

You can save yourself the expense of spaying or neutering by acquiring a cat that already has been altered. Kittens are adorable, and few people want to miss the fun and joys of this short-lived stage, but adult cats often cost less than kittens, simply because it is harder to find good homes for them. A grown American Shorthair can be an especially good bargain if you find one that is being retired early from a breeding program or the show ring. Typically, breeders keep so many cats in their catteries that they cannot afford to retain individuals that are no longer useful for breeding or showing. The reasonable solution is to place these retirees in good homes by selling them for less than the price of a kitten. In most cases, cats placed in this way are altered and up to date on their annual vaccinations prior to sale, saving the buyer these initial expenses.

Certainly, kittenhood holds special joys for cat lovers, but it can also be the most destructive stage. Kittens are not born knowing how you expect them to behave in your home. They have to be properly socialized and patiently taught not to climb your draperies and not to sharpen their claws on your couch. On the other hand, many adult cats are surrendered for adoption because of behavior problems related to their past care or lack of training. The most common behavior problems that result in cats being surrendered to animal shelters for adoption include house-soiling and destructive clawing.

In most cases, all you have to rely on is the seller's word and reputation, so ask questions and do your homework. Before you buy an adult cat, find out as much as you can about its history and health records.

Show Cat or Pet?

Breeders price and sell American Shorthairs according to whether they are pet-quality, breeder-quality, show-quality, or *top* show-quality. Cats in each category are purebred and fully registrable in the cat associations.

Pet-quality: American Shorthairs are the most affordable. If you have no real interest in showing or breeding American Shorthairs, and you simply want a nice pet, then a pet-quality American Shorthair is your smartest buy. You can reasonably expect to pay between $250 and $350 or more for a pet-quality American Shorthair, depending on availability, color, and geographic location. Pricing also depends largely on each kitten's bloodline, type, color, and markings.

The pet-quality designation in no way means that the cat or kitten is less healthy or less desirable to own than a show-quality animal. It simply means that, in the breeder's opinion, some minor cosmetic flaw may make the cat unsuitable for show ring competition. On the positive side, a pet-quality American Shorthair makes an ideal household companion, but at a lower cost than a show animal. Generally speaking, only judges, breeders,

Silver classic tabby kittens: American Shorthairs make fine companions, regardless of whether they are male or female, pet-quality or show-quality.

and other cat fancy enthusiasts familiar with the breed's show standard can tell the difference between a pet-quality American Shorthair and a grand champion.

Responsible breeders will usually sell their pet-quality American Shorthair kittens only with a signed agreement that the new owner will spay or neuter. To ensure that the agreement is honored, the seller may elect to withhold the kitten's papers, or registration slip, until the buyer furnishes a veterinary statement proving that the required operation has been performed. In this way, breeders aim to discourage unethical people from buying purebred cats at pet prices, breeding them for profit, and adding to an already overcrowded pet population.

Breeder-quality: American Shorthairs also fail to meet the show standard in some small way, yet they possess enough good qualities, in addition to their excellent pedigree, to produce potentially outstanding offspring. Breeder-quality kittens are typically priced in the middle range, selling for somewhat less than their show-quality littermates, but for more than a

pet-quality animal. Expect to pay around $500 to $800 for a breeder-quality American Shorthair. Again, pricing can vary and depends largely on each kitten's bloodline, type, color, and markings. To prevent indiscriminate breeding, some breeders will sell breeder-quality kittens only to other serious American Shorthair breeders, that is, unless the buyer signs an agreement to spay or neuter the animal.

Show-quality: American Shorthairs are the most expensive to buy, about $800 and up. Breeders consider show-quality kittens to be outstanding examples of the breed, based on the standard, and they anticipate that such kittens will perform well in the show ring. Few breeders will sell a top show cat to a novice; however, many will part with proven winners retired from breeding or competition, as long as the buyer agrees to spay or neuter the cat. More often, the breeder may neuter or spay the cat first, then try to place it. Because you can still show a spayed or neutered cat in premier or alter classes, acquiring an adult veteran show cat in this way can help you gain experience in the cat fancy arena, if that is your ultimate goal. This option also allows you the opportunity to acquire a high-quality show cat without the hassle of owning an intact, breeding animal.

When shopping for a show-quality American Shorthair, visit a few cat shows where American Shorthairs will be exhibited and note who the winners are. Since most exhibitors are breeders, talk to them about your intentions to buy, and collect their business cards. If you like a particular color of cat, this is a good way to find out who specializes in what colors.

Carefully study the pedigree of any kitten you consider buying. If the kitten comes from a line of champions or grand champions, those cats'

names will be prefixed by Ch. or Gr. Ch. The more grand champion titles that appear in the first two or three generations of a kitten's ancestry, the better the chances that the kitten, too, may grow up to be a winner. Although prices can vary widely, depending on availability and geographic location, it is not unusual for a top show-quality American Shorthair kitten to sell for several thousands of dollars.

Other Things to Consider

By now, you realize that acquiring a cat should never be an impulse decision. Because you are adding a new member to your family, you want to make sure you find a cat that will be a good fit for where you live and the way you live. Here are some other important points to consider:

Will your landlord allow pets? If you rent, your landlord may prohibit pets or require an additional fee, plus a pet damage deposit. Remember, as a pet owner, you are liable and responsible for any property damage or personal injuries your animal may cause.

Do you travel often? Animals need attention, so consider how much time you'll be able to devote to your cat. Also, if you travel often, can you afford boarding or pet-sitting fees? Or do you know someone who can care for your pet while you're away?

Are you or your family members allergic to cats? Many animals are surrendered to animal shelters each year because their owners cannot tolerate the severity of their allergy symptoms. Think about the people close to you who may no longer feel comfortable visitng your home because their asthma or allergies worsen in the presence of felines.

Your age and health: Certainly, most people expect to outlive their pets, but this is not guaranteed. Consider what would happen to your American Shorthair if you died suddenly or became incapacitated by an injury or illness. Too often, an animal faces neglect, abuse, or abandonment if the owner has not planned ahead for its care in case of an emergency. This is expecially true for pet owners who live alone. Give a trusted person advance instructions—and keys— to enter your property immediately and assume care of your American Shorthair if you should die suddenly or become disabled.

Reputable Breeders

If, after considering all of the above, your heart remains set on acquiring a purebred American Shorthair, the next step is finding a reputable breeder. The cat-registering associations can give you a list of breeders in or near your area (see page 92). If you live in or near a large city, attending cat shows that come to town is the best way to meet American Shorthair breeders. This allows you to see firsthand the quality of their cats. Cat fanciers' magazines list upcoming cat shows and publish breeder directories.

Some breeders advertise in the classified sections of newspapers and trade magazines or pin their business cards on bulletin boards at veterinarians' offices. Generally speaking, small-volume breeders are a good source from whom to buy. When you buy from a private breeder, you have the advantage of seeing what the mother, and sometimes the father, of your kitten looks like. If the location is within driving distance, you also can observe firsthand the environmental conditions under which the kitten was reared. Usually other cats from the same bloodline are present to give you a good

idea of what your kitten's appearance and temperament will be like when grown. Perhaps the greatest advantage in buying from a breeder, however, is the opportunity to establish a relationship with someone who has experience raising and showing your preferred breed.

Hallmarks of Reputable Breeders

Most breeders do not make a lot of money breeding cats, after figuring in the total costs of showing, health care, vaccinations, stud fees, food, supplies, and so on. They choose to breed because they love cats and because they gain a great deal of satisfaction from showing cats. Serious breeders are committed to improving the American Shorthair breed's aesthetic qualities in terms of genetics, temperament, and appearance. Those who show their cats must know the breed standard by heart, because they are striving to produce cats that best meet the ideals set forth in the written standard. Therefore, if you look for breeders who also show cats, you likely will avoid the less reputable backyard breeders who mate animals of questionable quality (and sometimes questionable lineage) and sell the offspring solely to turn a quick and easy profit.

Reputable breeders also take seriously their responsibility to coach others about becoming responsible cat owners. Each kitten they sell is typically accompanied by some form of owners' instructions, whether verbal or written, so that new buyers can start out properly caring for their kitten.

Unless they are selling to another breeder, reputable American Shorthair breeders generally stipulate in their written contract that a kitten is not to be used for breeding purposes. This means that you will not receive the kitten's individual registration form until you furnish proof that you've had your kitten spayed or neutered. Without this form, you cannot register your kitten, nor can its future progeny be registered. Some cat-registering associations even include space on their registration slips for breeders to indicate whether a cat can or cannot be used for breeding. If the *Not for Breeding* box on the form is checked and signed, the association will not allow kittens from that cat to be registered.

Questions a Breeder May Ask You

Responsible breeders always try to make sure their kittens are going to good homes, where they will be wanted, loved, and treated well. A conscientious breeder will ask potential buyers certain questions that reveal a lot about a person's attitude and knowledge about pet ownership, such as:

◆ Do you intend to keep your American Shorthair indoors?
◆ Have you owned cats before?
◆ Was your previous cat spayed or neutered?
◆ What did you feed your previous cat?
◆ Did you provide annual medical care for your previous cat?
◆ What happened to your previous cat?
◆ Do you own other pets now?

Such questions are not intended to make you feel intimidated, insulted, or defensive, so do not feel offended if a breeder interrogates you in this manner. Instead, recognize that you have been fortunate to locate someone who sincerely cares about the welfare of his or her cats. Breeders of this caliber feel that each kitten they raise represents a significant financial and emotional investment. They want to help other people become responsible pet owners and expand their general knowledge of cats. They also want you to consider your American Shorthair as a valuable investment, a cat that will become your priceless companion and a member of the family.

Questions to Ask the Breeder

Here are some questions you need to ask before the sales transaction becomes final:

◆ What cat association(s) does the breeder register with? Ask to see the pedigree.
◆ What vaccinations has the kitten or cat received? Ask for the dates when the shots were given.
◆ Is the kitten or cat certified free of feline leukemia virus (FeLV) and feline immunodeficiency virus (FIV)? Ask for copies of the kitten's health records.
◆ How much human handling has the kitten been accustomed to? Experts believe that kittens gently handled a little each day from about age three weeks on grow up to be more people-oriented and better socialized than those that have little or no human contact at all.

If possible, visit the cattery and note its overall cleanliness. With the number of American Shorthair breeders available

American Shorthair blue and white bi-color.

in the United States, finding one within reasonable driving distance of your home should not be too difficult; however, if the cattery is too far away for you to visit, ask to see pictures of the kitten and its sire and dam. Ask for references also, then call other people who have purchased the breeder's cats in the past and find out how satisfied they are with their animals.

More and more breeders are advertising via Web sites, so if you have access to the Internet, check out the list of Web pages listed on page 92, or use a search engine to find additional sites for the *American Shorthair Cat*. Visit Web sites for information about specific catteries and to see pictures of cats. Breeders can often send photos of their cats electronically, via e-mail, which is handy if you're interested in an out-of-state cattery. Also, many breeders can be located at Web sites such as the Breeders Referral List at *http://www.breedlist.com*.

When selecting a kitten, choose one that is active and playful, curious about its environment, and unafraid of humans.

Choosing a Healthy Kitten

Once you've found a reputable breeder, the next step is choosing a healthy kitten from the litter.

Check the following:

- The kitten you select should have good muscle tone, bright, clear eyes, and an alert, playful personality.
- A healthy kitten should not sneeze or show mucus discharge around the eyes or nose.
- The ears should be clean and free of dark, crusty wax. Head-shaking or ear-scratching may indicate ear mites or other infections.
- The anus should be clean and free of any signs of diarrhea.

- The kitten's coat and environment should be clean and free of fleas. To inspect the coat for fleas, rub your hand against the fur and look for fine grains of black dirt, which is really flea excrement. Flea signs are more prevalent behind the ears, on the back, and at the tail base, where the kitten cannot easily reach to lick clean.
- Tempt the kitten with a feather or ribbon and see how playful and relaxed it is around strangers. If it appears fearful, hisses at you, cringes from your hand, or, in general, seems unused to being handled, look elsewhere for a better socialized kitten.

Once you've selected a kitten, have your veterinarian examine it within a day or two after you take it home to help ensure that you've picked a healthy one.

Taking Your Kitten Home

Once you've selected a kitten, a responsible breeder generally will not let you take home an American Shorthair until it is at least 12 to 16 weeks old. By this time, a kitten has been weaned and litter-trained, is eating solid food, and has had most or all of its first-year's vaccination series. Kittens taken away from their original surroundings too young sometimes suffer from stress and have trouble adjusting to a new environment. Also, kittens that are weaned too young may have problems socializing, which can adversely affect their ability to bond with humans.

In addition, if your kitten must be shipped to you, it must be at least three to four months old to conform with most airline age requirements. The breeder usually helps with shipping arrangements, but you can expect to pay all costs, including the airline-approved carrier the kitten will be shipped in. Costs vary, of course, depending on the airline and the flight distance.

The Sales Agreement

When buying a cat or kitten, always negotiate a written purchase agreement before any money changes hands. A written sales contract describes all terms of the sale, including the purchase price and payment schedule, the breeder's health guarantee and any neuter/spay requirement. Contracts may vary from breeder to breeder, but, all agreements should spell out the buyer's option to return the kitten and get his or her money back if the kitten is found to be unhealthy or unsuitable within a specified period after purchase.

The breeder's contract also may require the kitten's new owner to give the breeder the first option to buy back the kitten, if the new owner can no longer keep it. Aside from stipulating whether an animal can be used for breeding, breeders may include other provisions in their contracts as well, barring the sale of the kitten to a pet shop or research facility or prohibiting declawing the cat. Be sure you read and agree to the terms in the sales contract.

Health records and vaccination certificates should accompany the sales agreement. To save money, some breeders vaccinate their own kittens, which is a legal practice, but, in areas where rabies shots are required for cats, the vaccine must usually be administered in the presence of a state authority, such as a veterinarian or an animal control officer, before a legal certificate can be issued. When shipping kittens by air, health and rabies certificates are typically required, depending on the destination and on the airline's regulations.

In addition to health certificates, the purchase price should include the kitten's papers and pedigree. Of course, depending upon the arrangements of the sale, the papers may be withheld until the buyer furnishes proof that the cat has been spayed or neutered.

The Registration Form

Registering a kitten enables you to show it in purebred competition classes, if you choose to do so (see Showing Your American Shorthair, page 89). Whether you intend to show or not, you want to buy an American Shorthair that is registrable. This means that the kitten's pedigree, or family history, can be verified and accepted by the cat-registering associations. An American Shorthair without papers may not be a purebred; after all, you have no proof of its parentage. Remember, you are paying for the predictable qualities that a certain bloodline offers. On the other hand, it's important to understand that papers alone do *not* guarantee the health or quality of a kitten.

Depending on the terms of your agreement, the breeder may give you the kitten's registration slip at the time of sale or mail it to you later. When you receive the form, simply fill it out with the name you have chosen for your American Shorthair. Complete the owner information section and mail the form with the proper fee to the association(s) in which the breeder registered your kitten's litter. The breeder will have completed the sections about your kitten's breed, sex, hair length, eye color, coat color, and so forth. Also, if the breeder has a cattery name, that name will be printed on the line where you write in the name you choose for your kitten. The cattery name will be part of your kitten's official, registered name, such as Cattery X's Little Miss Fluffy. While this may be the cat's full registered name, its common name used at home would be simply Fluffy.

Most forms direct you to select two or three names, in case your first choice has already been used by someone else. When the association receives the form, it will verify the pedigree information, approve your name selection, then send you back an owner's certificate.

A breeder may rightfully withhold the registration papers until you furnish proof that your American Shorthair kitten has been spayed or neutered.

BRINGING YOUR AMERICAN SHORTHAIR HOME

Planning and Preparing

Bringing home a new kitten is an exciting time for the whole family, but the sudden change to new surroundings may be somewhat intimidating from the new arrival's viewpoint. To make your American Shorthair's transition to its new home as comfortable as possible, a little planning and preparation are in order. Plan to make the event as quiet as possible. Give the kitten a few days to adjust to its new surroundings before inviting visitors over to see it. You'll also need to buy some basic pet supplies, such as a cat carrier, cat food, food and water dishes, cat litter, a litter box, and so forth. More on that later in this chapter (page 22).

Indoor vs. Outdoors

The first thing you need to decide before acquiring an American Shorthair is whether it's going to be an indoor or an outdoor cat. After investing a great deal of money in a purebred cat, it makes good sense to keep your American

While some people strongly feel that cats should be allowed to roam outdoors, experts say that cats kept safely indoors generally live longer, healthier lives.

Shorthair safely indoors. Also, many American Shorthair breeders will stipulate in their sales contracts that their cats must be kept indoors and allowed outside only with supervision. Still, some people insist on letting their cats roam freely because they believe that depriving cats of their outdoor freedom is cruel. It is true that cats kept indoors live longer, healthier lives as they are less likely to be exposed to diseases, plagued by parasites, hit by cars, attacked by dogs, bitten by wild animals, caught in wild animal traps, poisoned by pesticides, and harmed by cruel people.

By keeping your American Shorthair indoors, you can also expect to have fewer veterinary bills related to injuries from cat fights and similar mishaps. In addition, you will have peace of mind, knowing that your well-kept indoor cat has less of a chance of contracting illness or disease-carrying parasites, such as ticks, that could affect you or your family.

Keeping your American Shorthair indoors will also help ensure that it has the best opportunity to live out its full life expectancy. As long as you provide love and attention, your American Shorthair will be quite happy and well-adjusted living indoors. If you feel your American Shorthair *must* experience the outdoors, supervise outings in the yard, build an outdoor exercise run, or install a cat flap that provides safe access to a screened-in porch.

Once you've decided that your American Shorthair is going to be an indoor cat, you'll need to cat-proof your home, to make sure the environment will be safe.

A Shopping List

Now that you've surveyed your home and made it cat-safe for your new arrival, it's time to visit your local pet supply store and buy some supplies to help ensure that your feline companion will be comfortable in its new environment. Obviously, you'll need cat food, and these choices are discussed separately in the chapter on Feeding Your American Shorthair (see page 37). Here are a few other things you'll need to purchase before you bring the new arrival home.

Cat carrier: A suitable cat carrier is a must for your kitten to travel home in, as well as for future trips to the veterinarian or cat shows. Available at pet supply stores, and sometimes veterinarians' offices, carriers range from inexpensive fold-out cardboard boxes to the sturdier molded plastic ones. There are also wicker baskets and canvas totebag varieties. If your American Shorthair must be shipped by air, the airlines will specify the dimensions and type of pet carrier required in the cabin or in the cargo hold. Regardless of the carrier type you select, it should fasten securely and be well ventilated.

If you have more than one cat, each should have its own carrier for safe transport. Never put two cats together in a single carrier, even if they are best friends. The too-tight quarters and the stress of travel might cause them to fight and injure one another.

Feeding dishes: Every pet in the household should have its own feeding dish, so select one ahead of time for your new American Shorthair and decide on a feeding location. If you're concerned about other pets eating the newcomer's food, feed the kitten in a separate area, at least until it gets better adjusted to its new surroundings.

Stainless steel, ceramic stoneware, or glass dishes, although more expensive than plastic pet bowls, are generally easier to keep clean because they can be sterilized in the dishwasher without melting or warping. Ceramic dishes come in decorative varieties, but select only those sold for human use or labeled as lead-free; otherwise, you have no way of knowing whether the paints and glazes used on the dish contain harmful lead that may leach into your cat's food or water.

Plastic dishes are cheaper and come in a variety of colors and shapes. While many people use plastic with no problems whatsoever, there are two main drawbacks associated with plastic dishes that pet owners need to be aware of:

1. Some cats can become allergy-sensitive to the chemicals used to make plastic dishes. Allergy-sensitive cats may develop itchy bald spots and crusty sores around the mouth and nose.
2. Plastic dishes also tend to develop tiny pits and scratches over time, which can harbor bacteria and odors, despite diligent cleaning. The stale food odors that collect in these minute crevices may go unnoticed by the human nose, but the cat may find them offensive enough to refuse to eat. To avoid this drawback, simply replace plastic dishes with new ones periodically.

When selecting feeding dishes, keep in mind that most cats seem to prefer flat, shallow saucers or plates to deep bowls. Apparently, cats dislike having their sensitive whiskers rub the sides of the dish as they eat. In fact, some cats dislike this unpleasant sensation so much that they will resort to scooping out food morsels with their paws and eating off the floor.

Also, choose a weighted food dish that's heavy enough to not slide across the floor as the cat eats. Imagine how frustrating your meals would be if your plate kept sliding across the table every time you tried to take a bite.

Always wash feeding bowls after meals, and replenish water daily. In hot weather, American Shorthairs love a few ice cubes added to their water as a cool treat.

Self-feeders: Many owners like to leave out dry food for their cats to nibble on free-choice or *ad libitum* throughout the day. This practice is okay as long as you are careful not to over-feed (see pages 37–47, Feeding Your American Shorthair). Self-feeders, which handily dispense food from a bulk hopper as the cat dines, and self-waterers are convenient when you must go away overnight, but a steady overabundance of food supplied in this manner can create an overweight cat.

Self-waterers dispense water from an inverted bottle into a dish as the cat drinks. Be warned, however, that some American Shorthairs quickly discover how much fun it is to shovel out water or kibble with their paws simply to watch the liquid bubble or the food fall.

Litter boxes: Pet stores and mail-order catalogs carry a wide variety of litter boxes, from the basic open plastic models to the fancy ones with ventilated bottoms and pull-out trays. The more expensive ventilated designs allow air to circulate beneath a litter tray to help dry the urine. Covered litter boxes help contain odors

and give shy cats privacy, but some cats seem to dislike the confinement. For a kitten's shorter legs, start with a shallow litter box, then switch to a larger size as the cat grows.

Regardless of the kind of litter box you select, it's important to keep it clean, or the cat may stop using it if it becomes too soiled (see pages 76–78 for a discussion on dealing with litter box problems). You'll also need a litter scoop to remove solid wastes from the box daily. At least once a week, clean the box with hot water and refill with fresh litter. Keeping the box fastidiously clean and changing the litter frequently are the best ways to control litter box odor. Baking soda generously sprinkled over and stirred into the litter also helps control odor in close quarters. Or try one of several commercial cat box odor-control products available at pet supply and grocery stores.

For privacy, place the litter box in a quiet, undisturbed area of the house. Do not place it too near the cat's food dishes or sleeping quarters. Being fastidious creatures, cats normally do not like to eat or sleep near the place where they relieve themselves.

If you have more than one cat, provide each with its own litter box, and place them in separate locations, if necessary. Although cat friends will often share litter boxes, some more aggressive cats may chase others away in a show of dominance.

By the time your American Shorthair is old enough to leave its mother and go to its new home, it should already know how to use a litter box. The instinctive digging and covering behaviors come naturally to cats, so no training in that regard is necessary. Generally, all you have to do is show the kitten where its new litter box is. Do this when you first bring the

kitten home. Set it in the litter box and gently move its front paws in the litter in a scratching motion. Repeat this, as needed, after the kitten's first meal or two in its new surroundings, and it'll quickly catch onto the idea.

Cat litter: Litter selection is important, because if your cat doesn't like the texture or scent of the type you choose, it may refuse to use the box. Some cats dislike the perfumed or chemically treated pellets added to commercial litters for odor control. These additives may

Whether you have an indoor or outdoor cat, be aware that certain plants in your home or yard may be toxic to your cat.

please human noses, but cats seem to prefer their own scent. For really finicky felines, plain, untreated clay litter or sterilized sand may be better choices. Avoid using dirt from the yard or garden, however, as it may contain unwanted organisms, including the one that causes toxo-plasmosis (see page 31).

Some litter brands are designed to clump when moistened. These are popular and convenient, because the clumping factor makes it easy to scoop out urine along with solid wastes. This aids greatly in sanitation and odor control by leaving behind only clean, fresh litter, but there are two major concerns with clumping litters that cat owners need to be aware of:

1. Certain brands have an unfortunate tendency to stick to the cat's fur, although many of the manufacturers have worked to correct this problem.
2. Concerns have also been raised about clumping litters causing digestive blockages, if swallowed.

As a precaution, avoid using a clumping litter with young kittens, as they are more likely than adults to sample the stuff by tasting and eating it. Use it when your American Shorthair is grown, if you like, but inspect the fur on the backside, just to make sure that clinging clumps are not a problem with the brand you've selected.

Litter varieties touted as "trackless" are designed to stick less to a cat's paws, thereby reducing the number of granules tracked outside the box onto your carpets and floors. For greater economy, certain litter brands can be rinsed and reused, but most cannot be flushed down the toilet, so, to avoid ruining your bathroom plumbing, read product labels carefully.

Cat beds: Even when you provide a pet bed, most cats will choose their own sleeping places and alternate their napping sites on a whim. More than likely, the preferred spot will probably be *your* bed or your favorite chair. If you want to discourage your cat from sleeping with you, keep your bedroom door shut and provide the cat with a "cozy," a deep, round pet bed made of soft, plush fabric.

Transporting two cats in one carrier is not safe. The stress of transport may cause even best friends to fight.

Whether you buy a fancy pet bed from the pet store or simply throw an old blanket in a cardboard box, select something washable, because you want to be able to launder your cat's bedding frequently.

Scratching posts: Cats, even declawed ones, have an instinctive need to scratch and sharpen their claws on objects in their territory. This natural behavior not only removes dead nail and reconditions the claws, but also marks territory with scent from glands in the paw pads. The scent draws the cat back to the same scratching spot time after time. Obviously, this can pose a problem if your American Shorthair starts clawing your furniture. To help avoid this problem, provide your cat with an alternative scratching

Get your American Shorthair accustomed to using a scratching post at an early age. To introduce your kitten to the post, hold the front paws in your hands and gently move them back and forth in a clawing motion.

post. Pet stores sell carpet-covered varieties, or you may wish to build your own.

Some cats prefer bare wood or tree bark to carpet- or sisal-covered scratching posts. Others prefer a flat, horizontal surface to a vertical, upright post. If your cat has a strong preference either way, it may reject the post you provide, so be prepared to experiment with different varieties.

Carpeted cat trees that extend from floor to ceiling make attractive scratching posts and come in all colors to match any room's decor. Creative designs incorporate built-in perches and peekaboo penthouses for napping. Not only do they double as lofty sleeping quarters, they offer ample exercise and climbing opportunities for indoor cats. And because American Shorthairs like to be near their people, they are more likely to use a scratching post or climbing tree located in the room where you spend most of your time.

Before introducing your American Shorthair to its scratching post, make sure the post isn't wobbly and won't tip over as the cat claws it. Stability is the most important feature for you to consider when purchasing or building any scratching post. Obviously, if a flimsy, unstable post falls over and frightens or harms the cat, the cat likely will refuse to go near it ever again. The post also needs to be tall enough to allow a full-grown cat to stretch upward on its hind legs to its full length.

At an early age, introduce your American Shorthair to its scratching post. Simply show the cat the post, move its paws in a scratching motion, and praise lavishly when it does what you want. If necessary, rub some dried catnip on the post to entice your American Shorthair to play and climb on it. If the cat decides to try out your furniture, scold verbally by saying "*No*" in a loud, sharp tone. Or, squirt jets of clean water from a water pistol to startle the cat without harming it. Wait a few minutes, then carry the cat to its scratching post.

If clawing the furniture has already become an established habit, it will be harder to break, but not impossible. The recommended strategy is to make the inappropriate surface unattractive to the cat while, at the same time, offering a more appealing, acceptable substitute, such as a suitable scratching post. To discourage an undesirable scratching habit, cover the problem area temporarily with a loosely draped blanket, newspaper, wrapping paper, plastic bubble wrap, or sheets of aluminum foil. Then, as previously explained, consistently encourage the cat to use the acceptable substitute (see pages 75–76 for more information on scratching behaviors and declawing).

American Shorthairs are easy to train and readily learn to respond to voice tones and commands. If you are consistent and persistent in your methods, your cat should soon learn to restrict its clawing to the designated area. When disciplining your cat, use your voice, but never, *never* strike the animal with your hand, with a folded newspaper, or with any other object. Such abusive action will only make your cat fearful and distrustful of humans.

Cat toys: You don't have to spend lots of money on cat toys. Cats can amuse themselves with ordinary items you might use in your own recreational pursuits, such as Ping-Pong balls, golf balls, and tennis balls. Paper grocery bags are a great favorite, but avoid plastic bags, because cats, like children, may suffocate in them. Even a cardboard box with cutout peep holes makes an inexpensive cat toy that will give your cat hours of delight.

When selecting toys at the pet store, consider safety first. Choose only sturdy toys that won't disintegrate after the first few mock attacks. Remove tied-on bells, plastic eyes, button noses, and dangling strings that your cat could tear off and swallow or choke on during play. Never let your American Shorthair play with small items that could be chewed or swallowed easily—buttons, bows, hair pins, rubber bands, wire bread-wrapper ties, paper clips, cellophane, or wadded-up candy wrappers.

Supervise all access to fishing-pole-style toys with feathers, sparklers, and tied-on lures. These interactive toys provide great exercise in your watchful presence, but if left unattended, the attached line poses a potential hazard for swallowing, for accidental strangulation, or for wrapping too tightly around a limb and cutting off vital circulation. Always shut these types of toys safely away in a closet when you're not around to play with your cat.

String of any kind is a definite no-no for cats, so do not offer yarn balls or threaded spools as toys. If you use such items in crafts or hobbies, store them safely out of reach of your cat. Also, be careful of braided rugs or knitted afghans that might unravel if the cat plays with a loose end. Once a cat starts chewing and swallowing string or yarn, a considerable amount may amass in the digestive tract and cause life-threatening blockages or perforations. If you come home to find your cat with a piece of string hanging out of its mouth, *do not* attempt to pull it out; that can cause more serious, even fatal, injury if the string has already wound its way into the intestinal tract. Seek veterinary help immediately. Such a situation constitutes a true emergency. Surgery may be required to correct this condition, called *string enteritis*.

Catnip: Pet stores offer an array of catnip mice, catnip sacks, and other catnip-scented toys for your American Shorthair's pleasure. Some stores even sell planter kits so you can grow your own catnip at home. A member of the mint family, catnip is a perennial herb that many cats go wild over. When exposed to a catnip-scented toy, a cat will grip the object in its front paws, rub its face in the fabric, and roll ecstatically, kicking at the object with the back paws. Afterward, the cat lies sprawled on its back, as if drunk, and dozes off in a relaxed, trancelike state of bliss, purring loudly and contentedly.

The substance in the plant that elicits this response is called *nepetalactone*. The effect wears off in a short time and does not appear to compromise the cat's normal faculties; in fact, an unfamiliar sound will bring a catnip-intoxicated cat to its fully alert senses immediately. The catnip herb is not thought to be addictive or harmful to domestic cats but not all cats care for catnip. Some lack the gene that makes them respond to the plant's intoxicating effects, and they show no marked reaction when exposed to it.

Grooming supplies: You will need nail clippers, steel combs, and a natural bristle brush. For kittens, start grooming with small and medium-size steel combs, and save a wide-toothed one for use on adult cats. For flea control, purchase a fine-toothed flea comb. Once caught in the comb's closely spaced teeth, fleas drown easily when dipped in a pan of water. A fine comb also readily removes flea dirt deep in the fur. Talcum or baby powder helps remove oil and dirt from a cat's coat when sprinkled in and brushed out completely. For bathing your American Shorthair, select only pet shampoos labeled as *safe for use on cats.* Avoid dishwashing detergents, laundry

American Shorthair blue classic tabby and white. The gene that allows for this attractive white spotting pattern is not well understood.

American Shorthair silver mac tabby. The mackerel tabby pattern is characterized by narrow stripes spilling down the sides, resembling the ribs of a fish.

soaps, or human shampoos. *Never* use dog shampoos or dog flea products on cats, because the ingredients may be too harsh and concentrated for felines. In fact, it's wise not to expose your cat unnecessarily to the insecticide ingredients in flea shampoos for cats, unless your cat has fleas. For tips on grooming your American Shorthair, refer to page 81.

Window perches: These carpeted shelves that attach easily to windowsills give your indoor cat an eye to the outside world and provide a handy place to doze in the sun. To heighten your cat's pleasure, as well as your own, place a bird feeder or birdbath in view of the window, and your American Shorthair will be mesmerized for hours, as if watching "cat TV." You'll have just as much fun watching your cat watch the birds!

To prevent falls and escapes, make sure all window screens lock in place and are sturdy, tight, and secure enough to withstand a grown cat's weight if it lunges at a fluttering insect on the outside. Although cats are well known for

Cats and dogs often become good friends, especially if they are raised together.

their ability to right themselves in midair and land on their feet, veterinarians treat enough injured cats that fall or jump from upper-story windows to give the condition a descriptive name—high-rise syndrome.

Shorthairs and Other Pets

If you already have an adult cat or a dog, bringing a new kitten into their territory must be managed thoughtfully and carefully. American Shorthairs, being highly sociable and adaptable, generally get along well with other pets, but before exposing any newcomer to your resident cat(s), have it checked by a veterinarian and tested for parasites and contagious diseases, especially feline leukemia virus (FeLV) and feline immune deficiency virus (FIV).

While awaiting the test results, keep the new arrival isolated from your other pets, in a separate room or in a cage. This also allows time for the "house smell" to settle on the newcomer, which may help make the introductions less threatening. After a few days, remove the new cat from its separate quarters for awhile and let the resident pets go in and sniff the new scent. When the time seems right, allow the resident pets to see and sniff the newcomer, but supervise all contact for the first few weeks. Keep dogs on a leash during these first meetings so they won't chase and frighten the newcomer. Gradually increase the exposure time until the pets seem to settle down and become acquainted.

If you have rabbits, guinea pigs, birds, or other small pets, it's possible to achieve harmony among different species as long as you provide secure, separate living quarters for all and supervise any direct contact. While there have been reports of cats and pet birds striking up unusual friendships, it is never wise to leave an adult cat alone with uncaged birds or small animals of prey. Cats are natural predators, and it is neither fair nor reasonable to expect them to ignore or control their instincts under such circumstances. Likewise, if you have an aquarium, cover it with a lighting hood, so your cat won't be tempted to go fishing or swimming.

Although it's usually easier to introduce a kitten, rather than a grown cat, into a home that already has a feline, don't be dismayed if it takes as long as a month for the animals to accept each other and become friends. Cats are territorial creatures, and adding a newcomer to the environment means that new boundaries must be set. In time, the tension usually disappears; however, cats, like people, are individuals, and occasionally two turn out to be simply incompatible. Some breeders will agree to buy back a kitten if things don't work out in the new home. Just in case, always make sure your sales contract clearly states the terms of a return agreement.

Shorthairs and Children

Children find kittens irresistible, but they have to be taught how to handle them properly. Not only can a child injure a fragile kitten, but an animal frightened or annoyed by a child's unintentional roughness may defend itself by scratching or biting the child. To avoid such mishaps, teach your child that pets are not animated toys, and supervise all physical contact between small children and pets. If children pull on a cat's tail or ears, remove their hand and show them how to gently stroke the animal's fur. Explain to your children that loud screams and sudden movements may frighten the cat. Show them where cats like to be stroked most—under the chin, behind the ears, and on the neck and back. Explain that some cats do not like to be stroked on their stomachs and rumps, while others will tolerate it from people they know well and trust. Teach your children how to properly pick up and hold a cat.

Picking up a cat: The proper way to pick up a cat is to put one hand under the chest behind the forelegs and the other hand under the rump to support the rear legs and body. Cradle the cat in your arms against your chest. Your American Shorthair will let you know when it wants down. Although mother cats carry their kittens by the scruff of the neck, this method is not recommended. Carrying by the neck scruff can injure an adult cat if not done properly and should be reserved for emergency restraint. Even then, care must be taken to fully support the cat's rear legs and body weight with the other hand. Allowing the cat's full weight to dangle without such support can seriously injure those neck and back muscles. Also, never lift a cat by its ears or front paws.

Cats and Babies

Couples planning a family often ask whether they can keep their cat and still have a baby. We've all heard those ridiculous old wives' tales about cats sucking milk from infants' mouths and smothering them. Certainly, it's wise not to allow your cat to have unsupervised access to an infant, not because there's any truth to those silly old wives' tales, but because a baby's screams, cries, or jerky movements may frighten the cat and result in accidental scratching or biting. If necessary, install a screen door at the nursery entrance. Also, to keep cats out of the crib, consider buying a mesh crib tent. Baby supply stores sell these as well as cat nets that cover playpens and strollers.

Toxoplasmosis deserves a mention here, because it's one of those scary reasons well-meaning people bring up to convince mothers-to-be that their cats must go before a new baby comes. If you're planning to have a baby, get the facts first from your obstetrician and veterinarian. Studies indicate that most people already have a degree of immunity to the disease, but if a pregnant woman is exposed to it for the first time, birth defects can occur.

The disease is caused by a tiny organism called a *protozoan*. Cats get the disease by eating infected birds, rodents, or raw meat, then they shed the eggs in their feces. Humans can get the disease by handling soil or litter contaminated by the feces of an infected cat, but the majority of cases in humans are not the result of contact with cats, but instead, can be traced to people eating undercooked meat. A cat has to have the disease in order to pass it on, and tests are available to determine whether a cat is infected. If this issue concerns you, ask your veterinarian about testing your cat.

If your American Shorthair tests clean and is kept inside—never roams outdoors, never hunts, and never eats anything except prepackaged commercial pet foods—the chances of it contracting the disease are nearly nonexistent. To avoid exposing your cat to the disease, never feed it raw or undercooked meat.

If you become pregnant, discuss this important issue with your doctor. When you know the facts and observe sensible precautions—such as thoroughly cooking all meats before eating, washing your hands after handling raw meats, and wearing gloves when gardening or cleaning the cat box—there's generally no need whatsoever to give up your cat if you're going to have a baby.

As a general health precaution, keep indoor litter boxes and pet feeding bowls out of a crawling child's range. And cover children's outdoor sandboxes when not in use, so that free-roaming cats won't mistake them for oversized litter boxes.

Sometimes a cat may urinate on a baby's bedding or other items, marking them as part of its territory. Restricting access to the nursery will help prevent this normal but undesirable behavior. Spaying and neutering also tend to curb marking behaviors in cats (see pages 74–75 for more information on territorial marking).

To reduce accidental scratches, trim your cat's claws regularly. And of course, keeping your cat in good health, keeping its shots up to date and making sure it remains free of fleas, ticks, and other parasites, reduces the risk of disease transmission to yourself and your family. Contrary to those old wives' tales, cats and babies can coexist peaceably as long as you use some common-sense precautions.

Leash Training

A safe way to allow your cat to enjoy the outdoors is to teach it how to walk on a leash. Yes, cats can learn to do this, if you exercise patience and perseverance. Just don't expect a cat to ever *heel* with precision by your side the way a trained dog does. The best you can hope for is that your cat will learn to tolerate the leash well enough to lead you where it wants to go, but

one thing you should *never* do is tie a cat on a long lead and leave it unattended. Without supervision, a tied cat could become entangled and accidentally strangle or hang itself.

While American Shorthairs are intelligent and, therefore, generally easy to train, some cats take to walking on a leash better than others; much depends on individual temperament and willingness. To begin, select an adjustable nylon or leather cat harness and a lightweight leash. Most pet supply stores and catalogs market "figure-eight" harnesses designed specifically to restrain cats so that they can't slip free and escape. Do not use a choker collar designed for dogs. Also, cats can easily slip out of dog harnesses, so avoid those as well.

To begin leash training, accustom the cat to the harness by putting it on when you're home to supervise. Let the cat drag the leash freely behind it, but don't leave the cat unattended while doing this, because it might get entangled or accidentally hang itself. When the cat seems used to wearing the equipment, pick up the leash and, using a pull toy for enticement, gently coax it along for short distances. Praise lavishly when it goes in the desired direction. Practice indoors until your American Shorthair walks comfortably with you on a leash inside the house, then go outside for short walks in a quiet area. Until your cat adjusts to unfamiliar sights and sounds outdoors, take along a pet carrier, then, if something frightens the cat and causes it to struggle on the leash, simply pop it in the carrier for safety.

Kids and cats can be great companions, but young children must be supervised around animals and taught how to properly hold and handle a cat without hurting it.

Black American Shorthair: Halloween can be an especially dangerous time for black cats allowed outdoors.

Pet Identification

Because cats kept indoors occasionally escape and get lost in unfamiliar territory, it's a good idea to have some kind of pet identification on your American Shorthair. Even when a lost pet is picked up and placed in an animal shelter, it typically has little chance of being reunited with its original owner, unless it is wearing some form of identification. For this reason, and because some desperate people steal pets for sale to research laboratories, your cat is safer if it wears some sort of identification. While this simple precaution may not prevent your cat from being lost or stolen, a permanent ID may enhance its chances of recovery. Many laboratories will not buy a tattooed animal, and most shelters look for tattoos and other forms of pet ID.

Tattooing: A painless procedure provided by many veterinarians, tattooing involves inking the owner's Social Security number or a special code on the rear inner thigh. For best results, register the tattoo with a nationwide pet protection service that has a 24-hour hotline for tracing the number and finding the owner, no matter where the cat is found.

Collars and tags: These can be lost or removed, but they are better than nothing. A cat collar needs to have a stretch elastic or breakaway section, so the animal can escape without choking if the collar snags on a tree branch or other object.

Like collars, ear tags embedded in the ear like a tiny earring are better than no ID at all, but they, too, can be cut off, ear and all, by unscrupulous pet thieves.

Microchips: Animal shelters in many areas are using microchip technology to reunite lost pets with their owners. To use such an ID system, the owner has a veterinarian inject a tiny microchip under the skin between the cat's shoulder blades. The chip reflects radio waves emitted by a hand-held scanner, which reads the chip's code number. The owner then registers the code number in a computer database for tracking. Ask your veterinarian if such a system is available in your area.

We've all heard horror stories about cats that drink spilled antifreeze from puddles in the driveway, then get sick and die—but cats don't have to drink poisons to get sick. Nor are outdoor cats the only ones subject to potential harm. There are many indoor hazards, too.

Because cats are such clean creatures, they can ingest wax, bleach, detergents, and other toxic chemicals stored inside your home. All an unsuspecting cat need do is simply brush against a dirty storage container, or walk through a spill, then lick the offending substance off its paws and fur as it self-grooms. With this in mind, take an inventory of all household chemicals and other potential hazards in your home that a climbing, exploring cat might have access to, then, to make your home cat-safe, do the same things you would do to make it child-safe. Following are some suggestions:

◆ The risk of electric shock is one of the greatest hazards found inside the home. Chewing on electrical cords can result in burns and electric shock. To prevent this, tuck electrical and telephone cords out of reach under mats or carpets, tack them down, or cover them with PVC piping. Coating cords with bitter apple, bitter lime (available at pet stores), raw onion juice, or Tabasco sauce also helps discourage chewing. If electric shock does occur, disconnect the current before touching the cat, or use a wooden broom handle to disengage the cat from the wire. Even if the cat appears to suffer only minor burns to the tongue and mouth, consult a veterinarian immediately. Complications from electric shock may not be apparent right away.

◆ Keep window and drapery cords tied up and well out of reach, as a frolicking feline can become entangled in dangling cords and accidentally hang or strangle itself.

◆ Make sure all window screens are strong, sturdy, and secure enough to prevent a cat from pushing them out or falling through them. This is especially important if you live in a high-rise apartment building.

◆ Screen fireplaces.

◆ Store cleaners, laundry detergents, fabric softeners, solvents, mothballs, insect sprays, and all other household chemicals out of reach in securely closed cabinets.

◆ Keep perfumes, cosmetics, nail polish removers, and all vitamins and medicines, including aspirin and acetaminophen (highly toxic to cats), tightly capped and put away.

Cats can chew through electrical wires and get electrocuted. To avoid this hazard, tack or tape down electrical cords, tuck them out of reach, or run them through PVC piping.

- Put away pins, needles, yarns, spools of thread, artists' paints, and other hobby and craft supplies when not in use to prevent a curious American Shorthair from investigating them and accidentally swallowing something harmful.
- Consider children's toys that could pose potential dangers to a cat; for example, indoor basketball hoops over trash cans may trap a curious kitten that climbs or falls into the netting, causing accidental strangulation.
- Avoid using edible rodent and insect baits where your cat might get at them and get poisoned.
- Remove or secure all breakable items on tables, shelves, and bookcases that an exploring cat might knock over.
- Cover sump pumps and keep toilet lids down so that kittens can't fall in and drown.
- Before shutting the door of any major appliance, such as the dryer or refrigerator, check to make sure your cat hasn't jumped in unnoticed.
- Unplug small appliances when not in use. The dangling cords from a coffeepot or hot iron left unattended present a tempting hazard to a playful cat.
- Keep tight-fitting lids on all (indoor and outdoor) trash bins so that foraging cats won't get sickened by spoiled foodstuffs or injured by discarded razor blades, broken glass, or jagged tin can edges.

Don't leave out pills or loosely capped vitamin and medicine bottles that your cat could knock over and accidentally consume.

- Supervise all kitchen activities. With an American Shorthair in the house, no countertop is safe from exploring paws. If an inquisitive cat should leap up on the stove top when you're not looking, it can get burned accidentally by stepping on a hot burner or by sniffing a boiling saucepan or tea kettle.

While it's hard to think of everything, be creative when you are scanning your home for potential hazards. Keep in mind that whatever might harm a young child could also harm a cat.

FEEDING YOUR AMERICAN SHORTHAIR

Types of Cat Food

Of all the things American Shorthair owners can do to help ensure their cat's good health, providing good nutrition is probably the easiest, yet perhaps the most confusing. Many quality pet foods exist on the market today that are backed by years of careful, scientific research; however, the sheer number of product choices available can be overwhelming to the human consumer.

Commercial pet foods come in three basic types: canned, semimoist (also called soft-dry), and dry. Each type comes in a variety of flavors as well. Fortunately, with so many choices available, it is relatively easy to find good products that your American Shorthair enjoys and that are convenient for you to serve. Before you decide, however, consider the advantages and disadvantages of each type of food.

Dry Foods

Generally, dry foods are less expensive to buy and more convenient to serve. They are not as smelly as canned foods, and they can be left out

To help keep your American Shorthair healthy, feed it a complete and balanced commercial cat food formulated for your cat's specific life stage.

all day in a bowl for cats to nibble *ad libitum* or free-choice. Dry foods also may benefit cats by promoting better dental health. Although this issue has been widely debated, it is generally believed that the hard chewing action required with dry foods helps scour the teeth and gums, and thus aids in controlling ugly tartar buildup that can lead to gum disease and tooth loss.

Free-choice feeding has also been a matter of much debate. At one time, it was thought that nibbling on dry foods throughout the day predisposed cats to a lower urinary tract condition called feline urologic syndrome (FUS) by allowing the urine pH to become too alkaline; however, with improved food products now on the market, free-choice feeding is no longer the big issue it once was in this regard. That's because most cat food brands sold today have been reformulated with acidifying ingredients to better maintain urine pH levels within normal acidic ranges.

Leaving out measured portions for the cat to eat at will is now the method most often recommended in many dry foods' product feeding guidelines. Carefully measuring out each meal or each day's portion, as opposed to leaving out bulk amounts of dry food that could last for several days, is also a better strategy for preventing excessive weight gain in cats that tend to overeat.

Canned Foods

Usually more expensive than dry foods, canned foods contain more moisture than either dry or semimoist foods, making them a better choice for cats that need more water due to a medical condition. For cats that have missing teeth or sore gums due to dental disease, canned foods are also ideal because they require virtually no chewing. Finicky eaters also seem to prefer canned foods because canned foods often contain more protein and fat, making them generally more palatable to the feline taste buds.

Single-serving cans, although more expensive, result in less waste, because many cats will refuse to eat canned food after it has been refrigerated. Having evolved as predators, cats prefer their food warm, at the average body temperature of small prey animals or, at least, at room temperature, so always warm refrigerated leftovers before serving. When warming leftovers in the microwave oven, test the portion with your finger before serving to make sure it is not too hot. A cat that burns its mouth on hot food will probably refuse that type or variety the next time.

To avoid spoilage and odors, take up any uneaten portions of canned food as soon as the cat finishes eating.

Semimoist Foods

Semimoist foods typically come in soft-dry nuggets packaged in foil-lined wrappers or bags. These food products attempt to combine some benefits of the dry and canned types, making them an attractive, middle-of-the-road choice for the human consumer to use. Semimoist foods contain more moisture than dry foods, but they lack the odors of canned foods that human consumers so often find offensive. Also like dry rations, semimoist foods can be left out and fed free-choice without spoiling. Unlike dry foods, however, semimoist products are too soft to help reduce dental tartar. The convenience packaging is a major advantage, because the single-serving foil pouches take the guesswork out of controlled-portion feeding.

At one time, semimoist cat food products contained a preservative called propylene glycol, which is the same chemical used in safer antifreeze brands, as well as in many cosmetics, medicines, and alcohol beverages, but its use is no longer allowed in cat food products because it has been implicated in causing red blood cell damage in cats.

Popular vs. Premium Brands

Aside from the basic food types, cat foods are also packaged and marketed according to whether they are generic (economy brands), popular, or premium brands. While the cheaper generic foods, which are typically sold under a private label or store name, tend to be lower in quality and use poorer-grade ingredients, this is not always true. Sometimes it is cheaper for a manufacturer to simply stick a generic label on a popular brand and market it under a different name without changing the formula. Before choosing a generic brand, however, you should contact the manufacturer and thoroughly research the product ingredients.

The nationally advertised, popular name brand products are sold in supermarkets, while the more expensive premium brands are sold primarily through pet supply stores and veterinarians' offices. Other than price, some popular and premium brands may differ very little. There is no industry-regulated definition for what a *premium* or a *super-premium* product should be and no higher nutritional standard that premium pet foods must adhere to. These words are simply descriptive marketing tools.

The general assumption is, however, that premium foods contain higher-quality ingredients and remain stable in their makeup, whereas, popular brands are more likely to change recipe ingredients according to the current market cost and availability of those ingredients.

Premium products also are often marketed as being more digestible and *energy dense,* which means that a smaller amount is required per serving to provide the necessary nutrients. Another assumption is that the product research behind premium brands is more substantial, but many well-known popular brands are also backed by extensive research and years of experience on the part of the manufacturer.

Therapeutic diets, often called prescription diets, also are available through veterinarians for cats with special needs. These foods are formulated and dispensed by veterinarians specifically for certain health conditions, such as heart disease, kidney disease, intestinal disorders, or obesity. While most of these special diets come in dry or canned form, at least one for recurrent gastrointestinal problems is available in semi-moist form.

Life-Cycle Nutrition

Commercial cat foods are also formulated for specific life cycles of the cat, from kittens to senior citizens. That's because good nutrition is a relative term that depends a great deal on a cat's age, activity level, and current state of health. In other words, what's good for a kitten is not necessarily the best choice for an older cat, and vice versa. In fact, research has shown that certain nutrients consumed at too high or too low levels during early life stages may contribute to health problems in later life. This knowledge ended the old womb-to-tomb practice of feeding cats one food their entire lives, and ushered in a new era of life-cycle nutrition.

Today, life-cycle formulas that are scientifically tailored to meet a cat's nutritional needs during different stages of its life compete for grocery store shelf space. A pet food label states whether the product is formulated for growth and reproduction, adult maintenance, or for all life stages of the cat. Most manufacturers make a line of products geared to all three.

Growth and reproduction formulas are made specifically to satisfy the extra nutrient requirements of growing kittens and breeding or pregnant queens (female cats). Foods formulated for all life stages of cats meet these same requirements, because they must satisfy the range of nutritional needs for cats of all ages. Adult maintenance formulas are intended primarily for fully grown, nonbreeding, and generally less active felines; therefore, these foods do not have to meet the higher nutrient requirements of growth and reproduction formulas. For this reason, adult maintenance diets are *not* satisfactory fare for kittens or pregnant cats.

Feeding Kittens

For its first full year, your American Shorthair kitten needs a greater amount of high-quality protein for growth than it will require in adulthood. At least 30 to 40 percent of a kitten's diet should be protein. Select a kitten or feline growth formula designed to meet this extra need. Follow the feeding guidelines on the

package, adjusting the portions as needed. In general, you should let growing kittens eat as much as they seem to want.

While a high-quality food formulated for all life stages of cats is also adequate, dry foods formulated for growth and reproduction are usually molded into smaller morsels that make it easier for smaller mouths to chew. Kittens require more frequent feedings, but in smaller quantities, than adult cats. Newly weaned kittens need three or four feedings a day. By about age six months, two meals a day should suffice.

Feeding Pregnant Cats

· During periods of gestation (pregnancy) and lactation (nursing), breeding females ideally should receive a high-quality food formulated for feline growth and reproduction. Because foods labeled *For all life stages* of cats must meet the same requirements as growth and reproduction formulas, these products are also

Every cat in the household should have its own food dish and free access to plenty of fresh water.

sufficient. Because of the extra demand placed on their bodies, pregnant and nursing cats need more calories and high-quality protein to aid in fetal development and milk production. Again, follow the feeding guidelines on the package, adjusting the portions as needed. As with growing kittens, you should allow pregnant cats access to as much food as they want to eat.

Feeding Moderately Active Cats

Adult, nonbreeding cats need enough nutrients, fiber, and protein to satisfy their appetites, yet prevent them from getting fat. While a food formulated for all life stages of cats is fine for many adult felines—especially for the very active breeds—some cats tend to become overweight, particularly during middle age. Because

American Shorthairs tend to be moderately active in their adult years, a suitable commercial food formulated for adult maintenance may be an appropriate choice. Your veterinarian can best assess your cat's nutritional needs at any given age and recommend an appropriate diet.

Because adult maintenance formulas contain less protein than the growth and reproduction foods, or foods formulated for all life stages, they are unsuitable for growing kittens or pregnant cats. They are, however, adequate for a normal, nonbreeding adult's lower energy requirements.

Feeding Senior Cats

Foods labeled *For all life stages* are designed to meet the needs of all cats, from kittens to senior citizens; however, older, less active cats often require fewer calories, less salt, and less protein than these diets contain. Cats with special health concerns, such as kidney or heart disease, may also require one of several therapeutic diets available through veterinarians.

Other cats in their advanced years, although still in good health, may start growing thin because their bodies are no longer able to digest nutrients from their food as well as when they were young. To maintain their weight and condition, some of these older cats—as long as they're healthy and not suffering from kidney disease or other medical problems—

may thrive better on a highly digestible or energy-dense food to help make up for the nutrients their bodies are wasting. In some cases, a high-quality kitten or growth formula may even be appropriate for an otherwise healthy older cat. Such a choice would *not* be appropriate, however, if your veterinarian determines that your elder cat's kidney function has been compromised by old age or disease. Instead, the veterinarian may recommend a special food with only moderate levels of high-quality protein to ease the burden on the kidneys.

Remember, your veterinarian is the best judge of your American Shorthair's overall condition and dietary needs. Weight loss and other changes in your cat's condition need to be evaluated medically to rule out underlying causes, such as kidney failure or thyroid disease. Cats are generally considered seniors at age ten, but before your American Shorthair reaches the decade mark, ask your veterinarian to reassess your cat's dietary needs and recommend any appropriate changes in feeding routine.

Silver classic tabby American Shorthair adult cat and kitten. Because energy requirements change as a cat matures, kittens and adult cats have different nutritional needs.

Making Dietary Changes

With so many product lines and varieties to choose from, the important thing to remember is that no one perfect pet food exists for every cat and for every owner. That's why it may be necessary to change foods from time to time, as your cat's nutritional needs vary.

Although pet food labels provide helpful information, choosing a cat food solely by label contents or brand name is unwise. Instead, base your selection on how well your American Shorthair performs and maintains its overall condition on a particular food. Start with a high-quality kitten food that your breeder or veterinarian recommends, then, during annual checkups, as your veterinarian assesses your American Shorthair's condition, remember to ask about your cat's changing dietary needs as it reaches adulthood and matures into middle and old age.

Make recommended changes to your cat's diet gradually, over a period of at least a week or more. Sudden changes in diet or feeding routine may result in symptoms of gastrointestinal upset in some animals, or your cat may simply refuse to eat the new food. So, begin making any dietary change by mixing small amounts of the new food with your cat's current rations. Gradually increase the amount of new food as you decrease the amount of old food until the changeover is complete.

Finicky Eaters

Well known for their finicky eating habits, cats have a discriminating sense of taste; once developed, their taste preferences can be difficult to change. A cat fed the same type or flavor of food all its life may steadfastly refuse any sort of dietary change, even if its health depends on

it. To avoid creating finicky eating behavior, and to provide variety and appetite appeal, select two or three high-quality products your American Shorthair seems to like and use them interchangeably. Alternating a few varieties of cat foods and flavors from kittenhood on will go a long way toward preventing your cat from becoming addicted to one type of food.

Deciphering Labels

Pet food companies are required by law to supply certain nutritional information on their labels. We have already discussed the life-cycle formulas and what these disclosures on a cat food label mean. A pet food label must also disclose whether the food is formulated to provide complete and balanced nutrition. The word complete means the food has all the necessary nutrients a cat needs for good health. The word balanced means those necessary nutrients are present in the proper proportions. If the label doesn't say the food is *complete and balanced,* chances are it isn't.

Statement of nutritional adequacy: To prove that their products comply with nutritional guidelines set forth by the Association of American Feed Control Officials (AAFCO), and to substantiate claims of "100% complete and balanced" nutrition, pet food manufacturers must either adhere to a proven formula or subject their products to lengthy feeding trials with live animals. Of the two, feeding trials offer more assurance that the food is adequately nutritious, because the product has been test-fed to cats for a period of time under AAFCO protocols. Any product that has undergone feeding trials says so on the package. Look for the company's statement of nutritional adequacy, which should say something similar to: *Anima' feeding tests using*

AAFCO procedures substantiate that [this brand name] provides complete and balanced nutrition for the maintenance of adult cats.

Guaranteed analysis: The required guaranteed analysis must state on the label only whether minimum or maximum amounts of nutrients, in percentages, were met. It doesn't have to list actual concentrations of specific nutrients. The problem with not knowing how much a product exceeds the minimum requirement for a certain nutrient, such as protein, is that sometimes too much can be just as bad as too little, depending on the cat's age and condition. What that means is that, while foods formulated for *all life stages of cats* are designed to meet normal nutritional needs of cats of all ages, some individuals, particularly older ones or those predisposed to certain health problems, may get far more of certain nutrients than they need.

Ingredients list: Ingredients are supposed to be listed in descending order of predominance by weight, but this can be somewhat misleading. For example, meat may be listed first, leading the consumer to believe the product contains mostly meat, when, in reality, the summation of separately listed grains and cereals makes plant material the predominant ingredient. Some labeling terms are strictly regulated, while others are not; for example, the title wording of "Chicken for Cats," "Chicken Platter," "Chicken Entree," and so on, can have different meanings in terms of the percentage of chicken the product must contain. A good way to check specific ingredient amounts is simply to call the manufacturer's toll-free number on the package and ask for the data. Many companies have consulting veterinarians and/or nutritionists, and you can judge for yourself how willing and able they seem to be in sharing information and answering your ques-

tions. A manufacturer's long-standing reputation can offer some assurance that correct product standards are met and maintained.

Feeding Guidelines

As a guide to daily rations, follow the feeding instructions on the package and measure out the recommended portions. Keep in mind that feeding guidelines are based on average nutritional needs and, therefore, are not intended to be used as absolute amounts. Some individuals may need greater portions, some less. Because the amount of food your American Shorthair requires each day will vary with its age, weight, and activity level, you may need to adjust the rations to maintain optimum body weight and condition.

Generally speaking, a cat is at its optimum weight when you cannot see the ribs, but you can feel them without probing through thick layers of fat. Here again, your veterinarian can best judge your American Shorthair's overall body condition.

Most adult cats thrive on two meals a day, morning and evening. Others do well on a canned food breakfast, combined with ample dry food left out for free-choice nibbling. Whatever routine works best for you and your cat, your American Shorthair will feel more secure if you feed it at the same time and in the same place each day.

Homemade Diets

Because food is often viewed as a symbolic love offering, many people like to express their affection for their cats by cooking for them, but constructing a complete and balanced meal for

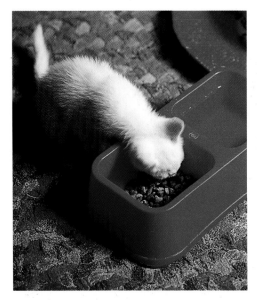

has shown that if a cat's food is taurine-deficient, the animal stands a greater risk of developing blindness or a heart muscle disease called dilated cardiomyopathy. Prompted by such findings, manufacturers began routinely adding taurine to their commercial cat food products in the late 1980s, and since then, reported cases of dilated cardiomyopathy have declined dramatically.

Because the feline diet requires a delicate balance of numerous ingredients to maintain proper body functions and cell growth, too much or too little can be harmful. For this reason, home-cooked diets should be fed only in rare situations, such as when a cat is suspected of being allergic to an ingredient common in commercially prepared foods. Even then, the makeup of any routine homemade feline diet requires close supervision by a veterinarian with some expertise in animal nutrition.

This does not mean, however, that your cat should never sample any tidbits of people food. On the contrary, such treats are fine on occasion, as long as you don't overdo it. Just keep the portions small, and don't make such offerings a daily habit, or your cat may begin turning up its nose at its own food. Remember, table scraps and people foods do not provide a complete and balanced diet for cats. Also, garbage is garbage, so *never* feed your American Shorthair scraps that you would not eat, and, do not feed bones, as these may splinter and lodge in your cat's throat or puncture parts of the digestive tract.

a cat from scratch is not as easy as it sounds. It is a chore best left to the experts. That's because cats are carnivores by nature, which means they must have protein from animal sources to stay healthy. They cannot adapt safely to a vegetarian diet, nor can they thrive solely on *people food.* Their nutritional needs are significantly different from those of humans, dogs, and other mammals.

Reputable pet food manufacturers budget substantial amounts of money for research to back claims that their products provide "complete and balanced" nutrition for the various feline life stages. Without expert guidance, the home-based chef cannot guarantee an adequate mix of proteins, carbohydrates, fats, vitamins, minerals, and amino acids essential for maintaining good health in cats.

One amino acid in particular, taurine, is indispensable, because the cat cannot manufacture this essential ingredient on its own. Research

Obesity

If you're not careful, offering too many treats or too much people food can result in an overweight cat. Obesity is probably the most common nutritional disorder among pets in the United States today. Moderately active or sedate cats that live in apartments and have little opportunity to exercise seem especially prone to developing this health disorder, but any cat can become fat if consistently overfed.

Obesity in cats can pose some serious health risks. The extra weight puts a strain on all organ systems and contributes to a shortened life span. Also, an overweight cat is a greater surgical and anesthetic risk.

While many cats with free access to food appropriately self-regulate their consumption,

Always keep plenty of fresh water available for your cat to drink at will.

others overeat out of boredom. When feeding dry food free-choice, it is best to measure and leave out only the recommended amount per day or per meal, depending on your feeding routine. Check the product's feeding guidelines for recommended amounts, and adjust the portions as needed to help your cat maintain its ideal body condition. Owners often unwittingly contribute to the problem of overeating by leaving out huge amounts of dry food that could last for days.

Many owners enhance their cats' waistlines by offering too many high-fat, high-calorie gourmet snacks between meals. While there's nothing wrong with offering your American Shorthair an occasional treat, remember to not overdo it. Also, don't substitute foods intended as treats for your cat's regular daily rations. Many commercial cat treats sold in stores are not labeled as *complete and balanced.* That's because they don't have to be, when they are intended only for intermittent use, and not for daily rations.

Some overweight cases may result from feeding cats together, which encourages competition. In addition, many cats tend to gain weight as they grow older, simply because they play less and need fewer calories.

Weight gain and weight loss also can be symptoms of serious underlying medical conditions, such as diabetes, thyroid disorders, and kidney disease; therefore, a veterinary examination is in order before you reduce your cat's feed or attempt to put it on any special diet.

Weight-Loss Diets

Your veterinarian can recommend an appropriate weight-loss method to suit your cat's particular situation. Some veterinarians prefer to use a good weight-reduction therapeutic diet, while others recommend continuing on the usual food, but cutting back the amount fed and eliminating all treats.

Therapeutic weight-reduction diets are nutritionally balanced but lower in calories to produce weight loss without creating other deficiencies. They are also higher in fiber to promote a feeling of fullness in the animal. If your veterinarian recommends a therapeutic diet, and you have more than one cat, you may have to feed the one on the special diet separately.

Whatever method is used to achieve feline weight loss, owner compliance is the key to its success. It's also important that any weight loss be gradual and that changes in diet or food portions also be accomplished gradually, over a one- to two-week period. Putting an overweight cat on a crash or starvation diet can result in a serious, potentially life-threatening liver disorder, called hepatic lipidosis.

Foods to Avoid

Do not feed your American Shorthair dog food; canine formulas do not contain nearly enough protein or taurine to promote good health in cats.

Vitamin and mineral supplements, unless recommended by a veterinarian, are not necessary when you feed your American Shorthair a nutritionally complete and balanced commercial cat food. To compensate for nutrient losses during processing, pet food manufacturers add vitamins and minerals to their formulas to supplement natural nutrients contained in the primary ingredients. So, if you add more through additional supplementation (unless necessary to treat a specific condition), the balanced proportions of certain nutrients that your cat is receiving in its food could actually become unbalanced. Be aware of the following:

◆ Do not feed raw meats, raw fish, raw liver, or raw egg whites. Meat alone is not a balanced meal and, if served raw, may contain harmful bacteria and parasites, including the organism that causes toxoplasmosis. Raw fish can cause a thiamine deficiency. Raw liver, if fed daily in large quantities, can cause vitamin A toxicity. Raw egg whites have an enzyme that can interfere with vitamin biotin absorption. An occasional cooked whole egg is okay, as long as it is well-done.

◆ Chocolate can be toxic to cats and dogs, so keep candies, desserts, and baking chocolate covered and out of reach.

◆ Alcohol is also toxic to cats, even in small amounts, so never, *never* let anyone give your cat alcohol.

Urinary Tract Health

Over the years, numerous dietary elements have been blamed for causing the tiny struvite crystals that can plug the feline urethra in FUS, a potentially life-threatening disease. (Some veterinarians refer to FUS as LUTD or FLUTD, for feline lower urinary tract disease, an umbrella term used to describe all disorders of the lower urinary tract.) The suspect list has included ash, magnesium, phosphorous, and calcium, among others. As each suspect ingredient was incriminated, major cat food manufacturers promptly reformulated their foods to reflect prevailing scientific research and to allay consumer concerns.

Current findings suggest that the overall mineral composition of cat food, rather than an excess of any single ingredient, determines whether the urine pH becomes too alkaline (too high), providing favorable conditions for crystals to form in the urinary tract. Magnesium content remains a secondary concern, enough to warrant restricting dietary levels when managing FUS. Reflecting this knowledge, specialty foods began to proliferate the market bearing label claims of *low magnesium, reduces urinary pH,* or *helps maintain urinary tract health.* Beyond these permissible statements, cat food manufacturers cannot claim that their products treat or prevent FUS, or any other disease, without approval from the Food and Drug Administration, because to do so would be touting the diet as a drug.

Today, most regular cat foods now on the market contain enough acidifying ingredients to help keep urine pH within safely acidic ranges.

An acid urine helps dissolve struvite crystals or prevents them from forming in the first place, and researchers have noted a decrease in struvite stones, along with an increase in similar stones composed of calcium oxalate. The obvious conclusion is that the recomposition of commercial diets fed to cats is at least partly responsible for both changes.

While studies clearly suggest that restricting magnesium and maintaining a slightly acidic urine may help prevent struvite-related urethral obstructions, such a diet is certainly not considered a cure-all for *all* cats, particularly if it has the potential to cause other problems. While the link between diet and urinary tract disease remains under investigation, the best advice is to consult your veterinarian before starting your cat on any special diet. Furthermore, if you suspect your cat may have a urinary tract problem, seek veterinary attention immediately. Dietary management may be only part of the necessary treatment (see page 58).

Water Is a Must

Water has been called the forgotten nutrient because its importance is often downplayed when discussing how to feed cats; however, keeping fresh water in a clean bowl available for your American Shorthair at all times is a must. Cats can concentrate their urine and conserve water when necessary, but like most other mammals, they cannot survive for very long periods without water.

Milk is no substitute for water, nor is it a complete and balanced diet for adult cats. Some adult cats, like some people, develop a lactose intolerance to milk and will experience diarrhea if they drink it.

KEEPING YOUR AMERICAN SHORTHAIR HEALTHY

A Health Concern to Owners

American Shorthair cats are a relatively hardy breed with few genetic flaws. Aside from the common diseases that can afflict all cats, there is at least one health condition that current and potential American Shorthair cat owners need to be aware of.

Hypertrophic Cardiomyopathy

While all cats, and even humans, can develop this heart muscle disease, medical literature notes its occurrence in certain breeds, including the American Shorthair, more so than in others. The disease, which causes the heart wall to thicken, is believed to be inherited and caused by a genetic mutation. For reasons unknown, the disease seems to occur more frequently in male cats during their young or middle adult years. Symptoms may include lethargy, difficulty breathing, appetite loss, exercise intolerance, and partial or total paralysis in the rear legs. The hind-leg lameness, although often mistaken by the owner to be a trauma-related injury, is actually the result of blood clots in the arteries that serve the rear limbs. Many cats with the disease develop heart failure and die within a few months after being diagnosed, although others with less severe cases can live longer and be managed with medications.

American Shorthairs are a hardy breed.

Researchers eventually hope to devise a genetic test that can be used to identify affected animals before they are used for breeding. This could one day help eliminate the disease, if all breeders complied. Until then, however, be sure to ask breeders about any incidences of hypertrophic cardiomyopathy that have shown up in their bloodlines *before* you purchase an American Shorthair kitten.

Choosing a Veterinarian

One of the most important decisions you will make as a cat owner is which veterinarian to visit regularly. Try to make this decision *before* you acquire your American Shorthair, because you will want to schedule a post-purchase exam within one or two weeks after you bring the newcomer home. Whether you choose someone in general veterinary practice or someone who treats cats exclusively, make sure you are comfortable with the way the veterinarian deals with you and your American Shorthair.

For example, at your first appointment, note whether you feel at ease with the way the doctor addresses your concerns and explains terms, procedures, or findings. Also, does he or she seem willing to take time to answer your questions and share information? If you're a first-time cat owner, you'll want to use this opportunity to ask for advice on care and nutrition. Many veterinarians view pet owner education as an important part of their job and will hand out brochures and wellness kits to new clients. Others show videos on everything from diet to dental care. It's important to establish a good rapport with your veterinarian and his or her staff, because their professional guidance will be a valuable asset to your ongoing education as a cat owner.

Keep the clinic's emergency number handy, in case your American Shorthair becomes ill or injured. Also, find out whether the clinic offers additional services, such as grooming and boarding, that you might want to use later.

Signs of Illness

With proper nutrition, regular veterinary checkups, good dental care, and routine vaccinations, you can reasonably expect your American Shorthair to live an average of 10 to 15 years. When illness does strike, however, you as the owner, must be prepared to recognize the signs and symptoms and seek veterinary care right away. By recognizing a problem early and seeking treatment, you can greatly improve your cat's chances of a full recovery.

Changes in appetite: Often, the first telltale sign that something is wrong is a sudden change in appetite. That's why any marked change in normal eating habits should be regarded with suspicion and carefully watched. If the problem doesn't resolve itself quickly, within 24 hours or so, report your observations to your veterinarian.

Changes in litter box habits: Likewise, sudden changes in toilet habits should be investigated for medical causes. If you notice that

your American Shorthair is missing the litter box, straining to urinate, urinating more often, passing bloody urine, or urinating in unusual places, suspect a lower urinary tract infection or blockage and seek medical attention right away (see page 57).

Other trouble signs: These include unexplained or rapid weight loss, increased thirst, frequent vomiting or diarrhea, coughing, sneezing, bleeding, staggering, swellings, panting, lethargy, lameness, coat changes, nasal discharge, bloody stool, crouching in a hunched-up position, hiding in unusual places, and difficulty breathing. The list is by no means complete. Because cats can succumb rapidly to illness, don't delay in seeking veterinary help at the first hint of trouble.

While it's wise to always keep your American Shorthair safely indoors, you should especially do so if you suspect an illness so you can observe it closely. Sick cats often seek seclusion in out-of-the-way places, and if you allow your cat to wander off, you may not find it again until the illness is too advanced to be effectively treated.

Annual Checkups

Adhering to a routine vaccination schedule and getting annual preventive health care checkups for your cat benefits both of you. Obviously, your cat will have a better opportunity to enjoy a longer, healthier life. And you can save money by preventing problems instead of treating them. The cost of aggressively treating a single serious illness can quickly surpass the money you spend on yearly physicals and routine booster shots throughout your American Shorthair's lifetime.

Vaccinations

Combined with good health care and nutrition, keeping your American Shorthair indoors can maximize its chances of living out its full life span. Certainly, an indoor cat is less likely to contract an illness from a free-roaming animal or to fall victim to other outdoor hazards, but keeping your cat indoors doesn't mean you can skip the routine vaccinations altogether.

Several infectious diseases common in cats are caused by airborne organisms that can waft into your home on a breeze through open doors and windows. Even your hands, shoes, and clothing can serve as transmission modes, silently tracking in deadly disease-causing organisms. Fortunately, highly effective vaccines exist to combat many feline diseases, and that's why it's important to keep recommended vaccinations current, even if your American Shorthair stays indoors all the time.

Passive Immunity

Kittens acquire maternal antibodies from their mother's first milk, the colostrum. This is called passive immunity, and how long it lasts depends upon the antibody level in the mother's blood when the kittens are born. Protection usually lasts from 12 to 16 weeks, but it may wear off as early as eight weeks. Because kittens are highly susceptible to certain infectious diseases, vaccination at about eight weeks is recommended to ensure that they remain protected; however, if maternal antibodies are still present in the kitten's system when it receives its first shots, those passive antibodies may render the vaccines ineffective. That's why shots for the common feline respiratory infections and feline distemper are repeated at about 12 weeks of age, to ensure that they "take," as well as to provide the kitten with continuous immunity as maternal antibodies wear off.

How Vaccines Work

Vaccines artificially induce active immunity by stimulating the production of antibodies against a specific organism. As long as the antibody level remains high enough in the body, the antibodies can attack and overcome a disease organism that attempts to invade. Because this protection wanes over time, your American Shorthair needs periodic booster shots throughout its lifetime to maintain an adequate level of antibody in the system.

Booster shots: Traditionally, veterinarians have given yearly booster shots to maintain adequate immunity. But recent studies suggest that immunity with certain vaccines may last much longer than once thought. This new knowledge, combined with heightened concerns about soft-tissue tumors occurring at common vaccination sites (see page 55), prompted some practitioners to revisit their views on vaccine protocol.

In 1997 an advisory panel established by the American Association of Feline Practitioners and the Academy of Feline Medicine studied the issue and recently set new guidelines, separating vaccines into core and noncore categories and recommending less frequent boosters for the core diseases, since immunity appears to last longer.

Core vaccines protect against severe or easily transmitted diseases and are recommended for *all* cats. The core diseases include rabies, feline distemper, and two upper respiratory illnesses, rhinotracheitis and calicivirus. Except for rabies, the core vaccines are typically combined into one convenient injection, to spare your cat the

Kittens' first shots are important because the passive immunity to disease these youngsters acquire from their mother's milk lasts only a short time.

discomfort of multiple needle pricks. According to the new guidelines, most cats should get core vaccine boosters once every three years; however, cats with a greater risk of exposure—those allowed outdoors, used for breeding, or frequently exposed to other cats, for example—may still need booster shots once a year, or as recommended by your veterinarian. In addition, state laws dictate the frequency of rabies vaccinations and should be followed accordingly.

Noncore vaccines are recommended for cats at highest risk of exposure to feline leukemia virus (FeLV), feline infectious peritonitis (FIP), chlamydia (feline pneumonitis), and ringworm. These vaccines are considered optional and should be administered based on the risk of exposure; for example, a cat kept indoors has less

chance of exposure to FeLV. However, a cat that goes outdoors, is frequently boarded, is used for breeding, has contact with other cats, or lives with a FeLV-positive cat has a greater chance of contracting the disease and needs the vaccine's protection. In addition, yearly boostering for cats receiving this protection is still recommended.

Vaccination Schedule

Any change in your cat's lifestyle, such as the addition of a new cat to the family, may require some changes in your vaccination program. At your cat's annual checkup, therefore, be honest with your veterinarian about how often your cat goes outdoors, even for short, supervised jaunts; how frequently it travels with you; whether you exhibit it in cat shows; and how often it is exposed to other cats. By knowing these details, your veterinarian can more accurately assess your cat's health risks and recommend an appropriate vaccination and booster shot schedule.

Establishing initial immunity: Most experts still agree that the *ideal* vaccination schedule begins with giving kittens their first combination core shot for upper respiratory infections and feline distemper at approximately six to eight weeks of age. Between eight and 12 weeks of age, the first in a series of two shots for feline leukemia virus (FeLV) may be given. At 12 weeks of age, another shot for upper respiratory infections and distemper is administered. Then, between 12 and 16 weeks, kittens get a rabies shot, plus the second shot in the FeLV series. A year later, all vaccinations should be repeated and thereafter followed up with periodic boosters on a schedule recommended by your veterinarian.

Side effects: Side effects from vaccines are minimal in most cases. Some cats experience mild lethargy for a day or two after receiving their shots. Your veterinarian can recommend an appropriate booster shot schedule for your cat. Depending on the circumstances, your veterinarian may recommend administering the vaccines separately and spacing them apart.

Feline Diseases

Feline Viral Rhinotracheitis (FVR)

Commonly called *rhino,* this serious upper respiratory infection that is caused by a herpes virus is often mistaken by the misinformed for a common cold. Symptoms include sneezing, nasal discharge, and crusty, watering eyes. Often, the cat stops eating. Immediate medical attention is a must.

Highly contagious, the disease spreads easily from cat to cat through direct contact with body secretions and contaminated objects, such as litter boxes, feeding bowls, or even human hands. Some cats show only mild symptoms and recover quickly, while others become progressively worse and may develop severe complications, such as eye ulcers. In some cases, the virus damages the throat, sinus, and nasal structures, leaving the cat prone to repeated bacterial infections in those areas. Rhino has a high mortality rate among kittens and older cats. Cats that survive the acute illness may become chronic carriers and, during stressful periods, will shed the herpes virus, making them a potential hazard to other cats in the household. The vaccine for this herpes virus is one of the core vaccines, and by far the most effective way to reduce the occurrence and severity of upper respiratory infections is simply to vaccinate all cats.

Feline Calicivirus (FCV)

Like FVR, FCV is a serious upper respiratory infection with similar symptoms, except FCV is more likely to progress to pneumonia. Painful tongue and mouth ulcers can make the disease particularly disabling, as the cat may refuse to eat or drink. Muscle soreness, exhibited by a stiff gait or limping, also may be

American Shorthair black smoke. Annual veterinary checkups and regular vaccinations can help your cat live a longer, healthier life.

present. Like FVR, some cats that recover from the calicivirus may become carriers. The best prevention is administering a core vaccine.

Feline Panleukopenia Virus (FPV)

Perhaps more commonly known as feline distemper or feline parvovirus, FPV bears no relation to the virus that causes distemper in dogs. The disease is destructive, highly contagious, and often fatal. Fortunately, it is less common than it once was, thanks, no doubt, to effective vaccines, which should be a core part of every cat's immunization program.

Without early detection and treatment, the infected cat becomes desperately ill. Onset occurs four to six days after exposure, and early signs may include appetite loss, depression, fever, and vomiting yellow bile. Because the virus often attacks the lining of the small intestine, the disease also is sometimes referred to as feline infectious enteritis. An afflicted cat will show signs of having a painful abdomen and may cry out pitifully if touched in that area. Sick cats have reportedly been observed crouching in a stiff, hunched-up manner over a water bowl, as if wanting to drink but unable to. A lowered white blood cell count (leukopenia) confirms the diagnosis and gives the disease its clinical name.

Feline Chlamydiosis

Sometimes referred to as feline pneumonitis, this respiratory infection is caused by an organism called *Chlamydia psittaci*. With respiratory symptoms similar to those in FVR and FCV, chlamydia infection often begins with weepy eyes and swollen eyelids. The disease can be quite contagious, especially among kittens; however, recent studies indicate that only a small percentage of feline respiratory infections in the United States are actually caused by chlamydia. For this reason, the vaccine is considered noncore, to be optionally administered, based on risk of exposure. As with the other types of respiratory illnesses, the best defense is routine vaccination, which can help lessen the severity of the disease should it occur.

Rabies

One of few feline ailments transmissible to humans, rabies occurs in nearly all warm-blooded animals. Skunks, foxes, raccoons, cats, and dogs account for most sporadic outbreaks in the United States. The deadly virus passes from an infected animal's saliva through a bite, open wound, or scrape. People bitten by a rabid animal must immediately undergo a series of injections in order to save their lives, for beyond a certain stage, the disease is inevitably fatal. Whenever a human life is at stake, an animal suspected of having rabies is humanely destroyed, and its brain tissue is tested to confirm the presence of the virus.

Once inside the body, the virus travels to the brain, where it produces two characteristic forms: furious and paralytic, or *dumb,* rabies. In the furious phase, cats exhibit personality changes that progress from subtle to severe. While symptoms can vary, normally affectionate and sociable cats may withdraw and hide. Aloof cats may become more loving, but in a few days, most infected animals become irritable and dangerously aggressive. Animals in this *mad dog* stage often act frenzied and deranged and will attack viciously without provocation. In the dumb phase, paralysis overtakes the body, starting with the face, jaw, and throat muscles. Unable to swallow its own saliva, the afflicted feline may foam at the mouth or, more typically, drool saliva that looks like strings of egg white. Eventually, the rear legs give way, and the cat can no longer stand or walk. Death soon follows.

Fortunately, regular vaccination easily prevents this merciless disease. Because of the threat to human health, the rabies vaccine is a core part of every cat's immunization program. In addition, most localities have laws requiring immunization of dogs and cats. To guarantee a certain immunity level, an initial rabies vaccine requires a booster one year later; thereafter, some regions permit boosters that do not need to repeated again for three years.

Without question, all outdoor cats should be immunized against rabies because of their potential exposure to infected animals, wild or domestic. Even if your American Shorthair stays indoors, keep its rabies immunization current in case it bites someone, or in case it escapes outdoors and risks exposure to a rabid animal. If your cat bites someone, certain quarantine procedures may apply, and you will certainly need legal proof of current immunization from your veterinarian.

Feline Leukemia Virus (FeLV)

First discovered in 1964, FeLV is a retrovirus that suppresses the bone marrow and the immune system, rendering its victims vulnerable to various cancers, such as leukemia, and other secondary ailments. Symptoms vary but generally include weight loss, anemia, poor appetite, lethargy, and recurring infections. An infected cat may seem healthy for years before finally succumbing to a FeLV-related illness. Testing is available to determine FeLV status with reasonable accuracy, although an occasional false positive or false negative result is possible. To help

prevent the spread of the disease, all cats should be tested to ensure their negative status before being introduced into a new household with other felines.

The first FeLV vaccine took about 20 years to develop. Initial immunity is usually established with two injections spaced about a month apart, then maintained by annual boosters. Although vaccination is considered a highly effective weapon against this devastating illness, recent research has raised concerns about a low incidence of tumors, called fibrosarcomas, developing at the injection sites of FeLV (and rabies) vaccines. While not caused by the vaccines directly, the tumors appear to result from a profound localized inflammation some cats experience, perhaps in reaction to the aluminum compounds used in the vaccine suspension.

As the matter remains under investigation, not all veterinarians recommend FeLV vaccination for *all* cats. Some recommend it only for cats at greatest risk of contracting the disease, which is why the vaccine is considered noncore, or optional. Also, veterinarians avoid giving the FeLV vaccine between the shoulder blades because the tumors are less operable there. As part of an effort to standardize vaccine sites, and thus help track adverse reactions, the FeLV vaccine is now generally given in the cat's left rear leg, while the rabies shot is given in the right rear leg.

In deciding whether to vaccinate your cat for the leukemia virus, keep in mind that FeLV is high on the list among the leading causes of death in cats. If your American Shorthair gets the disease, there is no cure. When discussing the preferred course of preventive care with your veterinarian, remember also that, according to the experts, the overall incidence of tumor development at the injection site is considered quite low, compared to the number of vaccines given. Unvaccinated cats face a far greater risk of developing fatal disease if exposed to the virus.

Cats allowed outdoors have the highest risk of FeLV exposure and certainly should be vaccinated. Others at risk include those living in multicat households and those exposed to outdoor cats, whether through direct contact or through screened windows. To be safe, any cat that comes into contact with other cats through breeding programs, at boarding kennels, or at cat shows needs protection against FeLV. Breeding toms and queens should be tested and certified free of the virus. Ideally, kittens should be tested before vaccination to rule out disease, because they can acquire the virus from an infected mother through the placenta or through the breast milk. If FeLV-positive, vaccination likely will neither help nor harm them.

Because the disease passes from cat to cat through bite wounds and prolonged casual contact, all FeLV-positive cats should be kept indoors and isolated from FeLV-negative cats, even vaccinated ones. There is no evidence to indicate that FeLV is capable of causing disease in people.

Feline Infectious Peritonitis (FIP)

This potentially fatal illness is caused by a coronavirus that spurs an inflammatory reaction in the blood vessels and body tissues. The disease strikes primarily younger and older cats and those debilitated by other illnesses, such as feline leukemia virus. Common signs include fever, lethargy, appetite and weight loss, and an overall unthrifty appearance. FIP typically takes one of two forms, wet or dry. The wet form involves fluid buildup in the abdomen and chest. An afflicted cat exhibits labored breathing, extreme depression, and a swollen belly. The dry form progresses more slowly and affects many organs, including the liver, kidneys, pancreas, brain, and eyes. Because symptoms are often vague, the dry form is more difficult to diagnose. The first FIP vaccine became available in 1991 and is given in the form of nose drops. Many veterinarians recommend it only if the exposure threat is high. The disease poses a greater hazard in catteries and multicat households, so discuss this vaccine option with your veterinarian.

Feline Immunodeficiency Virus (FIV)

Discovered in 1987, FIV is a retrovirus in the same family as FeLV and human immunode-

American Shorthair silver classic tabby and white.

ficiency virus (HIV), the virus that causes AIDS. Although FIV is sometimes called *feline AIDS*, it is important to understand that people *cannot* catch this disease from cats. FIV is a species-specific virus, meaning that it infects only cats and is not transmissible to humans or to other animal species.

The disease appears to be transmitted among cats mainly through bites. Because they often engage in territorial fighting, free-roaming males have the highest risk of contracting FIV. Cats kept indoors have the least risk, which is another sound reason to keep your American Shorthair safely indoors.

A test can confirm a cat's FIV status as positive or negative, although no cure and no approved vaccines currently exist. Once contracted, the disease persists for life, although a cat may remain healthy for months or years before its immune system weakens enough to allow secondary infections to take hold. Symptoms vary but usually include lethargy, weight loss, gum disease, and chronic infections. The best prevention to date simply involves avoiding contact with potentially infected cats, which is easily accomplished by keeping your American Shorthair indoors. Also, it's a good idea to have all breeding animals and all new cats coming into your household tested for FIV (and FeLV) to ensure their negative status, before exposing them to your American Shorthair.

American Shorthair red classic tabby.

Feline Lower Urinary Tract Disease (FLUTD)

The urinary tract collects and disposes of urine through the bladder and a tube called the urethra. In female cats, the urethra is short and wide, whereas, in males, this opening through which urine passes is longer and more narrow. For this reason, males are more prone to urinary tract blockages than females, although problems can occur in both sexes. In FLUTD, also called feline urologic syndrome, or simply FUS, tiny mineral crystals form in the lower urinary tract and irritate the internal tissues.

In response to this discomfort, the cat may repeatedly lick its penis or vulva and urinate in unusual places, such as the bathtub. Feeling an uncomfortable urgency to urinate, the cat may make frequent trips to the litter box. The cat even may strain or cry as it attempts to void. Some people mistake this straining to urinate for constipation. If you notice these symptoms, or if you see blood in the urine, take your American Shorthair to a veterinarian immediately. If the crystals are large enough, they may block the

urethra completely, creating a life-threatening emergency. If the cat cannot eliminate its urine, the kidneys may sustain irreversible damage from the backup pressure. Within a short time, toxic wastes can build up in the blood with fatal consequences. With prompt medical treatment, most cats recover; however, recurrences are common. Often, bacterial infections in the bladder or urethra complicate matters. The veterinarian may recommend medications and dietary changes to manage the condition.

While dietary factors are known to play an influential role in the disorder (see page 47), some veterinarians believe that disruptive and drastic changes in the environment or the household routine may detrimentally influence urinary tract health as well.

Internal Parasites

The most common internal parasites that plague cats include tapeworms, roundworms, and hookworms. An infected queen can pass certain worms to her kittens through the placenta and through the breast milk, so during your American Shorthair's first visit to the veterinarian, request a stool analysis, which unveils the presence of most worms. Because deworming drugs can cause toxic reactions, they should be administered only under veterinary supervision. An effective parasite prevention program includes keeping cats indoors, getting regular veterinary checkups, maintaining good sanitation, and controlling fleas, rodents, and other vermin.

Tapeworms: These are the most common internal parasites found in adult cats and are transmitted by rodents and fleas. During grooming, cats ingest fleas, which often carry immature tapeworms. Once ingested, the tapeworm larvae mature inside the cat's intestines, feeding on nutrients within and growing into long, segmented strands. When passed in the stool, fresh tapeworm segments look like grains of white rice and, upon closer inspection, may be seen moving. Occasionally, dried segments that look like tiny, flat seeds may be observed sticking to the hair around the cat's anus, even in short-coated cats like the American Shorthair. Left untreated, tapeworms rarely cause any outward clinical signs, but because they feed on the intestinal contents, they can rob the cat of important nutrients. For effective treatment, combine deworming agents with appropriate flea control measures.

Roundworms: Kittens get roundworms from their infected mothers or through contact with contaminated cat feces. Signs of parasitic infestation may include vomiting, diarrhea, weight loss, a potbellied appearance, and overall poor condition. Roundworms passed in vomit or stool look like white, wriggling spaghetti strands.

Hookworms: More prevalent in hot, humid areas, hookworms are picked up from soil infested with the larvae. Symptoms may include anemia, diarrhea, weight loss, and black, tarry stools.

Heartworms: These also occur in cats, particularly in humid regions, but they more commonly affect dogs; however, the incidence of this condition in cats appears to be on the rise, especially in certain high-risk areas where the mosquito, the host organism for heartworm disease, strongly prevails. Cats acquire the disease from the bite of a larvae-carrying mosquito. The larvae migrate to the cat's heart and pulmonary arteries, where they mature into adult worms. In most cases, a cat's normally functioning immune system mounts an attack and kills the larvae before they reach the heart; however, if one parasite survives to adulthood inside the cat, the cat may develop shortness of breath, coughing, and periodic vomiting. Once a cat is infected with heartworms, treatment can be risky. The medication used to kill adult worms can have serious side effects, so prevention is a much better choice. If you live in a humid, mosquito-plagued region, your veterinarian may recommend preventive heartworm medication for your cat, so be sure to discuss this option during your cat's regular checkup.

Lungworms: Acquired from contact with infected cats or from eating infected birds and rodents, lungworms migrate to a cat's lungs and cause a dry, persistent cough. Flukes, although uncommon, can be ingested by eating infected raw fish and other small prey. Cats allowed outdoors should be checked for worms during their annual physical checkups.

External Parasites

Fleas

Without question, fleas are the most common external parasites to plague cats and frustrate their owners. Easy to spot, these annoying insects leave behind evidence of their visits to the host in the form of "flea dirt," which looks like fine grains of black sand in the cat's fur. To inspect for flea dirt, rub your hand against your cat's fur along its back and near the neck and tail, and look closely at the skin for tiny black specks. Fleas feed on your cat's blood, which means the pepperlike granules deposited in the fur are really flea excrement from digested blood. If dampened, the tiny specks dissolve into bloody smudges. Left untreated, flea infestations can cause anemia from blood loss, espe-

Fleas can carry tapeworm larvae, which your American Shorthair may ingest as it grooms itself.

cially in kittens, and damage a cat's coat and skin from excessive scratching.

Even indoor cats are not immune to the scourge of fleas. Following the mere scent of a warm-blooded animal, these tiny but relentlessly bloodthirsty and biting insects can jump through holes in walls or window screens or ride in on a person's clothing or shoes in search of a suitable host. Once indoors, fleas lay eggs on the host and turn your American Shorthair's plush, dense fur into a virtual nursery for millions more. As the cat moves and scratches, the eggs fall off into your carpets, upholstery, and bedding, where they hatch into larvae. The larvae feed on debris among deep carpet fibers, an indoor environment that mimics their natural habitat—grass. Frequent vacuuming helps control this stage, but throw out the bag afterward, or the larvae will simply mature inside the bag and jump out.

American Shorthair cameo classic tabby.
Even indoor cats are not immune to fleas.

Flea-control products: Effective flea control used to require an arsenal of products designed to treat the pet and its environment at various phases of the flea's complex life cycle. This arsenal included sprays, dips, powders, flea collars, medicated shampoos, and room foggers, all targeted to kill or control fleas at the egg, larval, pupal, or adult stages. Often, these products failed to be effective when applied during the wrong life cycle of the insect and required repeating. They could also be potentially dangerous if used inappropriately or in combination with incompatible products. Even flea collars, although easy to use, posed a risk of strangling or choking, unless designed with elastic or breakaway sections to make them safer.

In recent years, flea control has become much easier and more effective with the introduction of some new one-spot products that are applied topically once a month. One such product is Advantage (imidacloprid). It comes in a small tube and is dabbed directly onto the cat's skin at the back of the neck once a month. A similar topical product applied in the same fashion is Frontline Top Spot (fipronil). The active ingredient in both products spreads across the entire animal and kills adult fleas by impairing the insects' nervous system, before they can lay eggs and before they can bite and irritate the cat.

An oral product called PROGRAM (lufenuron) is taken internally and must be mixed in the cat's food once a month. For this drug to work, fleas must bite the host and drink its blood. Once they feast on the cat's treated blood, female fleas living on the host will produce infertile eggs. Male fleas are unaffected. By interfering with the flea's reproductive cycle, the drug is useful for controlling indoor infestations, but, because of the way the drug must work, it obviously is not a cure-all for cats that suffer from flea allergy dermatitis, an allergic reaction to flea bites (see the section on cat allergies, page 62).

These once-a-month products are available through veterinarians. Although somewhat expensive, these products pay for themselves in terms of effectiveness, convenience, and ease of application. They spare you the hassle and your cat the trauma of repeated dips, baths, powderings, and sprayings.

When choosing any type of flea control product, there are several important rules to remember:

◆ Select only products labeled as safe for use on cats. Products intended for use only on dogs often contain medications that are too strong, sometimes even fatal, when applied to cats.

◆ Read the product label directions carefully *before* using the product on your cat. If you have questions, don't guess. Call your veterinarian and clarify any concerns you may have about using the product.

◆ Never use any product on a kitten or a debilitated cat without veterinary approval.

◆ Be careful to avoid potentially toxic combinations. Some products do not mix and match well, so before using more than one flea control product, or before using any product with other medication your cat may be taking, ask your veterinarian if the ingredients can be used together safely.

Ticks

Besides fleas, cats sometimes play host to ticks, lice, and mites. Ticks burrow their heads into the skin and suck blood. They often go unnoticed until they swell large enough to be felt as a bump in the cat's fur. If you discover one, remove it promptly by grasping the tick's body as close to the cat's skin as possible with tweezers. (Because of the risks to human health, experts recommend wearing rubber gloves while removing ticks, and thoroughly washing your hands afterward.) Pull the tick straight out (without twisting) with firm, gentle traction, then drown the insect in alcohol. Make sure you've extracted the entire insect, head and all; otherwise, a piece left behind may cause an infection under the skin, requiring veterinary attention.

Because some ticks carry Lyme disease, which humans can catch, take precautions to check for and control them if you choose to allow your American Shorthair outdoors under supervision. A tick can manage to hitch a ride even when its host experiences only short forays into the grass. Some products used to control fleas also repel or kill ticks, so ask your veterinarian to recommend one.

Lice

Uncommon in well-kept, healthy cats, lice look like white specks (nits) stuck to the fur. Clipping the coat and bathing with a medicated shampoo, available through veterinarians, gets rid of them.

Mites

Being microscopic, mites are harder to see, but signs of their presence include itchiness, hair loss, crusty sores, scaly dandruff, and body odor. Before recommending appropriate treatment, a veterinarian needs to identify the specific mite variety through examination.

The most common mite found on cats is the ear mite, which lives in the ear canal and produces a crumbly, dark brown, foul-smelling, waxy discharge. While healthy ears are clean and pink inside, a waxy, brown buildup in your cat's ears may indicate ear mites. Other signs include head-shaking, holding the ears to the side of the head, and repeatedly scratching at the ears. Prompt treatment prevents spread to the inner ear, where an infection can lead to hearing impairment. Symptoms of inner ear infection, such as staggering and loss of balance, require immediate medical attention. Because ear mites are contagious, other cats and dogs in the household may need treatment as well.

Skin Problems and Allergies

Ringworm

This itchy skin disorder is not caused by a worm at all, but rather by a fungus. Signs include scaly skin and patchy hair loss. Because people can catch this skin infection from cats, prompt veterinary treatment and disinfection of pet bedding are essential. Treatment may include clipping the coat, bathing the skin, and administering topical or oral medications. An optional vaccine is available to prevent ringworm, but veterinarians generally recommend it only if exposure risk is high, such as in households where ringworm has been a past problem. Discuss this option with your veterinarian if it is a concern.

Flea Allergy Dermatitis

Some cats are so allergic to flea saliva, that the bite from a single flea will send them into a frenzy, scratching, biting, and licking to get at the culprit. The severe itching lasts long after the flea feeds and departs, so you may never even see one of these nasty parasites on your pet. Such sensitivity can lead to an uncomfortable and unsightly skin condition in the cat called flea allergy dermatitis. Besides itchiness, symptoms include hair loss, patchy redness (called "hot spots"), and scabby, crusty sores on the skin. In addition to appropriate medications dispensed by your veterinarian to relieve the itching and skin problems, aggressive and diligent flea control measures help lessen the condition's severity and occurrence. A preferred choice would be a topical one-spot, once-a-month flea control product that kills adult fleas before they have a chance to bite the cat (see the section on fleas under External Parasites, pages 59–61).

Other Cat Allergies

Cats can be allergic to a host of other things in their environment besides fleas. Like people, cats can develop allergies to pollen, weeds, grasses, mold spores, house dust, feathers, wool, insect stings, drugs, chemicals, and food ingredients. Instead of sneezing, watery eyes, and runny noses, however, cats' symptoms more likely involve itchy skin, face, and ears. Typical warning signs include compulsive rubbing against furniture or carpet and excessive scratching, licking, or chewing at itchy places. Gastrointestinal symptoms like vomiting and diarrhea also can occur, particularly if the allergen, or allergy-causing substance, is ingested in a food or drug. Redness, crusty skin, and hair loss around the nose, mouth, and face suggests a food allergy, or possibly an allergy to plastic feeding dishes. In the latter case, replacing plastic dishes with lead-free ceramic or stainless steel ones offers an easy remedy.

Unfortunately, most allergy cases are not so simple. Testing exists, but allergies remain difficult to diagnose. Treatment varies widely from patient to patient, depending on the cause and symptoms, and may include antihistamines or allergy shots. Recovery can take a long time, and because allergies usually persist for a lifetime, owners must commit to avoiding or reducing the allergen in the cat's environment for as long as the animal lives.

Dental Care

Cats are not prone to getting cavities, but they are susceptible to gum disease, which can eventually lead to tooth loss. Dental disease can also silently compromise your cat's immune system and overall health by allowing bacteria to leak into the bloodstream from pockets of pus

To give a cat a pill, grasp the head gently with one hand, placing your thumb and index finger on the cat's cheekbones. Tilt the head back slightly, then gently pry open the jaws with your other hand. Drop the pill as far back in the throat as possible.

around sore, infected gums. Normal, healthy gums are pink, but diseased gums are tender, red, and swollen—signs of gingivitis (inflamed gums) caused by plaque and tartar buildup. Left untreated, this condition causes the gums to recede gradually and the teeth to loosen.

Bad breath is a cardinal sign of dental disease, but a cat with dental problems may also have difficulty eating because its teeth and gums hurt. As a result, it may lose weight and condition. A cat with sensitive teeth also may flinch when you try to stroke the side of its face. The best way to prevent such discomfort is to regularly brush or rinse your cat's teeth with oral hygiene products designed for use in animals. Also, from time to time, you may need to have your American Shorthair's teeth professionally cleaned. For this procedure, the cat is anesthetized, and the veterinarian uses an ultrasonic scaler to blast away the ugly, brown tartar and polish the teeth.

Medication

Getting your American Shorthair used to having its mouth opened and handled will make it

much easier for you to give it oral medications, should the need arise. Otherwise, the ordeal is likely to be a two-person job, with one person holding the cat while the other administers the medicine. Pills and liquids (see page 64) are the most common forms of medication you will likely have to administer, but whether your cat's condition calls for oral medications, injections, eye ointments, ear drops, or force-feeding that you must do at home, ask your veterinarian to explain and demonstrate the best method of application. Make sure you understand how and when to administer any medication before you attempt to do it yourself, and know what to expect in terms of recovery time and side effects.

After placing the pill as far back in the throat as possible, hold the cat's mouth shut and gently stroke its throat to encourage swallowing.

Never give your American Shorthair any drug or over-the-counter painkillers meant for humans. Tylenol and similar products that contain an ingredient called acetaminophen are especially lethal to cats, even in small amounts. Aspirin products can also be deadly. While certain products made for humans can be used on cats, the dosage, in many cases, must be diluted or carefully controlled and monitored, so never try to medicate your cat with herbal remedies, over-the-counter medications, or any other product not specifically labeled as safe for use on cats, without seeking veterinary advice first.

Pills

To restrain a struggling cat, wrap its entire body in a large towel, leaving only the head sticking out. To medicate, grasp the cat's head with your thumb and index finger on its cheekbones and tilt back the head. Using your other hand, gently pry open the jaws with your forefinger, drop the pill as far back into the back of the throat as possible, then hold the cat's mouth shut with one hand and stroke its throat with your other. The stroking motion encourages the cat to swallow.

Liquids

To administer liquid medication, tilt the head back slightly, insert an eyedropper or syringe (without needle) into the corner of the mouth, and gently squeeze in a few drops at a time, allowing the cat time to swallow. Do not squirt the medication into the cat's mouth too quickly or too forcefully, because the cat may accidentally inhale the liquid into the lungs, which could lead to pneumonia. Hold the animal's mouth shut and stroke the throat until the cat swallows.

Some liquid medications can be mixed in the cat's food, if they are not too bitter tasting. Cats can easily detect medications added to their food and usually eat around the edges or refuse the food altogether. Sometimes, lacing the drug with tuna oil or concealing it in strong-smelling, fish-flavored canned food works. When adding medication to food, make sure your other animals do not consume it.

Preventing Hair Balls

Cats, even shorthaired ones, can swallow a lot of loose hair as they groom themselves, particularly at the height

Two healthy and curious American Shorthairs, silver and brown classic tabbies.

of shedding season. Normally, this creates no problem; the hair simply moves through the digestive tract and gets eliminated in the usual way. Occasionally, however, too much hair accumulates in the stomach and is vomited back up as a hair ball. In more serious cases, the hair may form a large mass further along in the digestive tract, causing a blockage and requiring an enema or even surgery to remove. Signs of a blockage include refusal to eat or regurgitating food shortly after eating.

Hair balls are soft, tubular masses of ingested hair. Just before a cat spits up a hair ball, it will crouch low and cough a few times in a dry, hacking, wheezing manner. Sometimes the cat will sway its head from side to side as it coughs. This is distinctly recognized as the hair ball cough. As the cat prepares to vomit, it will crouch and convulse its whole body in waves before ejecting the material onto the floor. Vomiting a hair ball is usually no cause for concern, unless it becomes too frequent, in which case you need to offer some remedy.

Regular grooming is the easiest and cheapest way to prevent hair balls. Brushing and combing your American Shorthair helps remove the loose, dead hair it would otherwise swallow.

There are several petrolatum-based hair ball pastes available through veterinarians or at pet supply stores. To administer, squeeze a ribbon of paste onto your finger and entice the cat to lick it, or place an amount on the cat's tongue or paw. Another option is to dab some plain petroleum jelly (Vaseline) on the top part of your cat's front paw to lick off. These products help lubricate the hair mass so that it expels more easily.

Grass also seems to act as a purgative to help cats expel excess hair from the stomach. You can grow a fresh supply of grass indoors for your cat, and most pet stores sell kitty grass kits specifically for this purpose.

Euthanasia and Pet Loss

The unfortunate part of pet ownership is that cats don't live as long as people do. The average life span for an American Shorthair is about ten years, although with better nutrition and veterinary care available, many cats are living longer. Eventually, however, all cat owners have to let go and say good-bye.

Although difficult and painful, the decision to euthanatize (humanely put to death) a cat is sometimes the last and kindest gift we can offer a long-time companion suffering or debilitated from illness, injury, or old age. An anesthetic overdose administered by a veterinarian simply "puts the cat to sleep" without pain. Some veterinarians allow owners who request it to remain with the cat during the brief procedure, and many help handle cremation or burial arrangements.

For many people, losing a cherished cat companion causes as much trauma and heartbreak as losing a human loved one. This is not surprising, since the grieving process for pets is essentially the same as it is when we lose a human partner. The loss is especially intense when our pets have shared our daily lives more closely than our relatives or human friends.

When the inevitable does happen, giving another cat a good home is a beautiful way to honor your deceased friend's memory. Some people want to get another cat right away, while others feel a need to let some time pass. Another cat will not replace the one you lost, but when you feel ready, you can build a new relationship with another cat that will be as uniquely special, joyful, and rewarding.

Be Observant

Cats often conceal illness or pain, but observant owners can detect subtle behavior changes that cue them that all is not well. Early injury and disease detection can greatly enhance the odds of full recovery. Set aside time once a week to assess your cat's overall condition. Make a practice of inspecting your American Shorthair for white teeth, pink gums, clean, pink ears, clear, bright eyes free of discharge, clean fur free of flea dirt, and a firm body free of lumps, bumps, and tender spots. By doing so regularly, you are more apt to notice anything out of the ordinary.

Be Prepared

Once recognized, the key to successfully coping with any emergency is to be prepared for it. Always keep your veterinarian's emergency number handy. In addition, assemble the following items in a first aid kit:

- a blanket or towel to wrap your cat in for warmth and safe restraint
- gauze pads and strips for bandaging
- hydrogen peroxide antiseptic (it's fresh only if it bubbles) to clean wounds and induce vomiting

- antibiotic ointment, such as Neosporin, for superficial wounds
- tweezers, handy for removing foreign objects from paw pads or from the throat, if the cat is choking
- waterproof pouch to hold ice for controlling swelling and bleeding
- scissors and adhesive tape
- artificial tears or sterile saline eye rinse to flush foreign material from eyes
- rectal thermometer, pediatric size

Control Bleeding First

If an injured cat loses too much blood, it may go into shock and die before you reach a veterinary clinic. To control bleeding, cover visible wounds with gauze pads or some clean material and apply gentle, direct pressure over the site for several minutes. Do not attempt to splint or straighten fractured limbs, as this could cause more damage.

Transport Properly

Never pick up an injured animal by placing your hands under the belly. This will only worsen chest or abdominal injuries. If the cat is lying down, approach it from behind, slide one hand under the chest and one hand under the rump, and gently place it

in a pet carrier or on a blanket for transport. If the cat is crouched, grasp the scruff of the neck with one hand, place the other hand under the hips and rear legs for support, and cradle the cat in your arms. If the cat struggles, wrap it in a large towel or blanket, leaving only the head sticking out. Remember, no matter how gentle your cat is, it may bite or claw you if it's in pain. Position an unconscious cat on its side for transport and cover it with a blanket to keep it warm.

Accidental Poisoning

If you suspect your cat has ingested a potentially hazardous substance, call your veterinarian immediately. Do not induce vomiting unless an expert advises it. Some substances can cause more harm when vomited back up. When advised to induce vomiting, administer a small amount of hydrogen peroxide or warm salt water by mouth with an eyedropper. If you know what poisonous substance was ingested, take the package or a sample with you to the veterinarian.

For 24-hour assistance, seven days a week, call the National Animal Poison Control Information Center, operated by the University of Illinois. The hotline number is

(800) 548-2423. The service charges a flat fee for each initial case, payable by credit card, but followups are free. Those with short questions and those not wanting to use credit cards may have a per-minute fee added to their telephone bill by calling (900) 680-0000.

Certain medications and flea products cause some cats to salivate a little immediately after application. In many cases, this is no cause for concern, and the reaction subsides after a minute or two; however, if your cat begins salivating *heavily* after you've applied a topical flea preparation to its fur, or if it staggers or shows other unusual signs, rinse the substance off right away and call your veterinarian. Don't use the product on your cat again.

Similarly, if your cat's coat or paws become contaminated by bleach, pesticides, paint products, household cleaners and disinfectants, oil, tar, antifreeze, or other potential poisons, wash off the offending substance immediately. If necessary, clip away the affected fur. If the coat appears to be heavily saturated, or if you believe the cat may have already licked some of the substance from its coat or paws, seek veterinary help.

Removing Foreign Objects

If the cat is salivating, gagging, and pawing at its mouth, it may be choking on a foreign object in its mouth. Frequent culprits are bones, toothpicks, or staples stuck between the upper back teeth. Cats in this predicament often become quite frantic and, in their frenzied state, may claw or bite anyone who tries to help them. Transporting the animal to a nearby veterinary clinic for emergency assistance is usually the best approach, but if you feel you can do so safely, attempt to open the mouth and gently pull back the tongue for a better view down the throat. If you can see an obstructing object, use tweezers to gently extract it. If the object does not readily dislodge, make no further attempt to remove it without veterinary help. You may do more harm than good. Never poke tweezers into the eyes or ears; foreign objects lodged in these areas are best removed by a professional.

Heatstroke, Frostbite

Heatstroke and frostbite require immediate medical attention. To prevent heatstroke, never leave your cat in a parked car, not even for a few minutes, not even with the windows cracked. Temperatures inside a car quickly climb too high for safe tolerance, even on mild days. With only hot air to breathe, your American Shorthair can quickly suffer brain damage and die from heatstroke. Signs of heat stress include panting, vomiting, glazed eyes, rapid pulse, staggering, and red or purple tongue. Cool the body with tepid water, wrap in wet towels, and transport to a veterinary clinic immediately. To prevent frostbite, keep your cat indoors and avoid overexposure during cold weather.

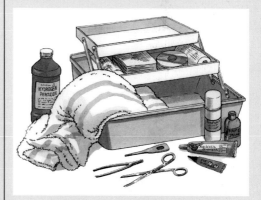

Be prepared for emergencies by keeping the following items handy in a first aid kit: towel, gauze pads, hydrogen peroxide, syrup of ipecac, antibiotic ointment, tweezers, ice pack, scissors, adhesive tape, saline eye rinse, and an infant-size rectal thermometer.

UNDERSTANDING YOUR AMERICAN SHORTHAIR

Body Language

Cats may not be able to speak our language, but like many animals, they are masters of body language. A simple flip of the tail or the flick of an ear can have specific meaning in "feline-ese." For example, when a cat walks toward you with ears pricked forward and tail held high, with just the tip slightly bending forward, it's saying, "I'm feeling good today, thank you, and it's great to see you!"

At the sight of a stranger, or a strange cat, however, your cat's behavior may change dramatically. When confronted by an adversary, for example, a timid or submissive cat crouches, lowers its ears, and drops its tail. A frightened or defensive cat can make itself appear as large as possible by arching its back and fluffing its fur out fully. An angry cat also crouches low, but its stance and tail action differ from that of the submissive cat. With ears flattened, muscles tense and ready to spring to action, the angry cat appears poised to attack. The flicking of its tail from side to side clearly signals a warning—"Back off!" If that posture fails to get the message

These kittens play and roughhouse to hone the skills they will use as adults.

across, a loud hiss or a low, drawn-out growl leaves no doubt that an attack is imminent.

Cats also have an extensive repertoire of mews and meows, which they use to communicate eloquently with their feline and human companions alike. As an American Shorthair owner, you will have a unique opportunity to learn these vocal sounds and to observe the subtle nuances of body language. In time, you'll become quite adept at interpreting your cat's moods and emotions.

If you're fortunate enough to share your life with two or more cats at one time, you'll have the pleasure of watching them engage in mock battles and move through a series of "attack" postures, all purely for fun. Cats that know each other well often play and roughhouse in a seemingly ferocious manner, yet they generally keep their claws sheathed and seldom injure each other during these encounters. Kittens, especially, play this way, and by doing so, hone the skills they will use later in stalking and hunting prey.

In a real confrontation, however, two cats may remain tense and still for several minutes, usually until one makes a strategic withdrawal. Being sensible, intelligent creatures, cats generally observe good territorial manners and avoid unnecessary "real" fighting, unless they're competing for dominance, territory, or mates; however, when a real fight does ensue, avoid getting in the middle of it physically, or you may get clawed or bitten. Instead, to break up a cat fight, clap your hands sharply and speak loudly and sternly, or make a loud, startling noise by banging on some appropriate object handy in the surrounding environment, such as pots or pans, for example. Squirting water on the cats sometimes works, too, but do not throw any objects directly *at* the cats.

Vocal Language

Mews and Meows

American Shorthairs have an extensive vocabulary of meow sounds, as do all cats. Perhaps recognizing that humans are not quite as adept as other cats at interpreting "feline-ese," cats often combine vocal sounds and body postures when communicating their needs to the owner. A typical communications exercise might involve leading the owner to an empty food bowl, and when no food is immediately forthcoming, resorting to plaintive mews. Generally, the more urgent the request, the louder the meow.

According to the intonation, a cat's meow can express many moods and needs. For example, a loud, throaty howl, or an urgent yowl, usually demands investigation. It may mean your cat is in distress—maybe it's gotten accidentally shut in the bathroom or a closet. Females in heat belt out a particularly annoying yowl that can rattle the senses. And mother cats (queens) chirp softly, in a most comforting way, when calling to their kittens.

In time, you'll begin to understand the meaning of your cat's personal repertoire of vocal sounds and body movements. What's more, you may even start talking back, all the while swearing that your American Shorthair understands every word you say. Sharing this secret language is an integral part of the bonding process between cats and humans. People who never take the time to observe and learn these mannerisms miss out on an experience that can be quite emotionally satisfying.

Ideally, you will come to feel that no one else can understand or care for your cat as well as you do. Most important, you will be able to recognize, before anyone else, subtle changes in your American Shorthair's mood and behavior that can be important clues that all is not well as far as your cat's health is concerned (see page 50).

Purring

The most universally recognized and beloved feline sound of all, the purr, is also the most mysterious. Experts still puzzle over the exact mechanism that causes or enables cats to purr. Most believe the sound is produced by vibrations in the larynx, or voice box, as the cat breathes in and out. By whatever means, cats obviously can control and produce the sound at will.

But *why* cats purr is even more mysterious than how. Even kittens as young as two days old can purr, but why nature endows them with the ability to do so at such a young age remains unknown. Perhaps the purr is a special form of bonding and communication between the mother cat and her young. This theory seems highly plausible, given the fact that, for human caretakers, cuddling a purring cat can help relieve stress, promote a mutual sense of well-being, and strengthen the human/feline bond. Perhaps by purring in the presence of a caretaker, cats are responding as they would to a "parent cat," communicating that all is well with them.

Of course, there is a long-held belief that cats purr to express contentment, when they feel happy, secure, warm, and well fed, but they've also been observed purring when nervous (at the veterinarian's office), upset, sick, hurt, or hungry. Remarkably, they've even been known to purr while dying. As a result, the generally accepted theory is that cats purr not only to express pleasure, but also to calm and comfort themselves when faced with adverse circumstances.

Your Cat's Senses

Under natural conditions, cats are nocturnal predators, as they evolved to be. Much of the mystery associated with them results from the unique anatomy that endows them with their special nighttime hunting prowess. Throughout the ages, the cat's mastery of the night has sparked awe and fear, as well as envy, in the human soul. A cat's five known senses are far superior to ours. Understanding how your American Shorthair perceives its world through these highly developed senses helps explain many behaviors that seem incomprehensible otherwise.

Sight

As primarily nocturnal hunters—creatures on the prowl for prey animals that come out mostly at night—cats possess excellent night vision. A special layer of cells behind the retina, called the *tapetum lucidum,* makes a cat's eyes appear to glow in the dark. These cells act like a mirror, reflecting all available light back onto the retina and giving the cat its exceptional ability to see well in low-light conditions. While cats can see much better in dim light than

humans can, they cannot see in total darkness. They also have poor color vision.

Cat eyes: The feline pupil can also dilate much wider than the human's pupil, thus allowing the cat's eye to collect light more effectively in dim conditions. A cat that feels threatened, frightened, or defensive will dilate its pupils to see better over a wider area. Of course, the cat's pupil works the other way, too. On sunny days, the pupils constrict to vertical slits to block out bright light.

Well suited to hunting and stalking, a cat's eyes are also especially adept at detecting the slightest movements made by small prey animals. Many prey animals have evolved with the instinct to freeze in place and remain perfectly still when threatened by the nearby presence of a predator, but a stalking cat will crouch patiently for long periods, staring at seemingly nothing, until its camouflaged prey finally reveals its whereabouts with barely a twitch in the grass.

Another special characteristic of the cat's eye is an opaque third eyelid, called the nictitating membrane, which helps protect and lubricate the eyeball. Although usually not visible under normal conditions (except occasionally when the cat is sleeping), the third eyelid may protrude from the eye's inside corner if the eye gets injured, irritated, or infected. The appearance of this white, filmy membrane over the eyes also occurs with some diseases and warrants a veterinary examination if it persists beyond an occasional blink.

Smell

Cats possess an acute sense of smell, far superior to a human's sense of smell, but not as good as that of dogs. When two cats meet on friendly terms, they typically engage in a ritual of sniffing each other about the head and anal

Cats have exceptional night vision.

areas, where scent glands exude a vast data-bank of personal information. Among cats, this behavior is the equivalent of the human hand-shake and hello.

A cat may also greet a human friend in similar fashion, jumping in the person's lap, sniffing the face, then turning with tail in the air to present its rear end for examination. In cat body lan-guage, this posture means, "Howdy, partner! Gee, it's good to see ya!" Faced with this situation, an appropriate human response in kind would be a gentle back scratch at the base of the tail.

Jacobson's organ: Like many other mam-mals, cats have a special scent mechanism, called the vomeronasal or Jacobson's organ, which adds a different dimension to their ability to detect and identify odors. Located in the roof of the mouth behind the incisor teeth, this spe-cial organ actually allows them to taste odor molecules. When using the Jacobson's organ, a cat curls its upper lip back and, with teeth bared and mouth partially agape, sniffs the air deeply through both nose and mouth. This gri-mace, often mistaken for a silent growl or a snarl, is called the *flehmen response.*

Many animals display the flehmen response during territorial or mating rituals. Cats can often be seen displaying flehmen when examin-ing urine and scent marks left by other animals. Researchers believe the special vomeronasal organ gives mammals an edge on finding mates by helping them sort out sex-related scent hormones called pheromones.

Taste

Specialized cells on a cat's tongue enable it to detect the chemical components of food as they are dissolved in the mouth by saliva. These taste buds send signals along nerve pathways to the brain, where taste identification actually takes place. Taste tests suggest that cats can distinguish between salty or sour foods, but they cannot taste simple sugars. According to the experts, this means that cats generally don't like sweet or sugary foods, although we've all heard tales to the contrary. In all likelihood, a cat that craves sweet treats is probably attracted by the good taste that results from high fat ingredients, but not necessarily the sugar.

The food with the greatest appeal to the feline palate is, of course, meat. Being naturally evolved predators, cats like their meat served warm, at room temperature or as near the body temperature of most small prey mammals as possible—not straight out of the refrigerator.

Touch

There's a common saying that if a cat's whiskers can pass through a small opening, the cat knows the rest of its body can fit through and follow. While this may be more fancy than fact (especially since obesity is such a common problem among today's house cats), it is true

American Shorthair blue classic tabby. With tail raised and ears pricked forward, this cat exhibits a keen interest in its environment.

that whiskers are highly sensitive tactile organs. Cats use them to touch and gauge the size of prey caught in their paws, to sense and avoid objects in dim light, and to detect vibrations and changes in their environment. For these reasons, *never* clip your American Shorthair's whiskers.

Hearing

Cats not only see and smell better than humans, they hear better than we do, too. Because their normal prey typically emits high-pitched sounds, cats' ears are tuned to frequencies well beyond the range of human hearing. Cats also have the apparent ability to selectively tune out what must be to them a cacophony of deafening noise in the normal household. They can sleep soundly in front of a blaring TV, snooze through the dishwasher's rinse cycle, and continue catnapping while the vacuum cleaner runs—but try sneaking open the refrigerator door for a snack, and your cat will come running from the farthest end of the house to see what's cooking. Even from the soundest sleep, a cat can be instantly alert when it hears something of interest, swiveling its ears toward the source and peering intently in the direction of the sound.

Cats also quickly learn to recognize the source and meaning of certain sounds; for example, chirping birds mean a possible meal is nearby. This associative ability extends from the hunting ground into the household, and after the first time or two, your American Shorthair will come running to the buzz of an electric can opener, the whisk of a pop-top lid, or the opening of the refrigerator door. And if you consistently call your cat by name each time you feed, it will quickly learn its name, and perhaps even come when called!

Balance

The cat also possesses an extraordinary sense of balance. If a cat rolls off a windowsill and falls in an upside-down position, a balance mechanism in the inner ear enables the cat to

rotate its forehand first, then the hindquarters, so that it automatically rights itself in midair and lands on all fours. This remarkable ability is known as the righting reflex. The cat's supple and flexible spine also contributes to its maneuverability in free-fall. But even with these impressive assets, cats that fall from great heights can still sustain fractures and other serious injuries. In fact, veterinarians see so many of these types of injuries that they've classified them under a special name—high-rise syndrome.

Territorial Marking

Rubbing

Cats have an endearing way of lovingly greeting their owners by rubbing against their legs, but the gesture is not merely an expression of affection—it is a means of territorial marking. By rubbing against furniture and other objects, cats leave behind scent from glands around their faces, mouths, and tails. Humans can't smell the scent, but other cats can. The message means, "I was here first, and this territory is mine!"

Cats will routinely travel the boundaries of their territory to inspect and refresh these scent markers. Your American Shorthair views you as an integral part of its territory, and each time it rubs against you, it is marking you with its scent and reaffirming "ownership." In addition, the mingling of your smell on the cat's fur helps identify you as a member within its circle of friends, so, in a sense, your cat is really saying,

A balancing mechanism in the cat's inner ear enables the animal to right itself in mid-air during a fall.

"You belong to me!" when it greets you by rubbing against your legs.

Spraying

Less endearing is the feline habit of spraying urine to mark territory. Although males are more prone to this behavior, females sometimes do it to communicate their reproductive status, especially when in heat. Spaying and neutering—operations that eliminate the reproductive function in cats—tend to curb this undesirable behavior, but both sexes, whether whole or altered (commonly referred to as "fixed"), may occasionally resort to spraying when engaged in a dispute with another cat over territory or dominance. For this reason, the problem is more likely to occur in multicat households, particularly in overcrowded conditions.

When a cat sprays, it generally stands, rather than squats, with its back to a vertical surface and with its tail straight in the air. The tail quivers as the cat squirts urine to mark the wall, drapery, or furniture leg. (For tips on dealing with unwanted spraying behaviors, see the section on House-soiling, pages 76–78.)

Clawing

When a cat scratches the arm of the couch, it is not misbehaving. Like spraying and rubbing, this action, too, is an instinctive territorial marking behavior. The cat is actually marking the scratched object with scent from glands in its paws. The cat is also fulfilling an instinctive need to keep its basic defense weaponry—its claws—sharp and trim. Similar to filing fingernails, the in-and-out action on wood or rough fabric helps strip away the dead, outer layers of the claws.

Outdoor cats can often be observed marking and sharpening their claws on the trunks of trees. For an indoor cat, this perfectly natural feline behavior can become a problem when the scent that's left behind on your furniture, combined with an apparent preference for the spot, continues to draw the cat back to the same site to claw until the couch arm becomes a shredded mess. You cannot eliminate this instinctive need to claw, but you can modify it and redirect it by providing your cat with an alternative scratching post, a suitable substitute for the tree trunk an outdoor cat uses (see below and pages 25–27).

Destructive Clawing

Scratching posts: While it may take a little time and patience to persuade a cat to use a scratching post instead of the couch arm, doing so is the best way to avoid destructive clawing habits, particularly when you start training early, before an undesirable habit develops. Once established, inappropriate clawing habits can be difficult to break, so begin teaching your American Shorthair kitten to use a scratching post as soon as you bring your new companion home.

Vinyl nail caps: Once a destructive clawing habit becomes firmly entrenched, one humane alternative for dealing with the problem is to glue vinyl nail caps onto a cat's freshly trimmed claws. These caps, which can be purchased through veterinarians, give the nails a soft, blunt tip and help prevent snags in carpets, furniture, and drapes. The major drawback to this method is that the vinyl caps have to be reapplied every four to six weeks, as the nails grow. The application is simple, however, and owners can purchase take-home kits and learn to manicure their cats' nails themselves. Ask your veterinarian to demonstrate the product. Vinyl nail

When a cat rubs against furniture or other objects in the home, it is performing a natural territorial ritual, marking the piece with scent glands around its face and head.

caps are not recommended for outdoor animals because they inhibit a cat's ability to climb.

Declawing

Declawing is the least desirable alternative for dealing with destructive clawing and should be considered only as a last resort after other methods have failed. Banned in some countries, this controversial procedure is still performed in the United States by veterinarians who consider it a viable option over having to euthanatize the cat because of destructive behavior or surrender it to an animal shelter for adoption.

The declawing procedure involves putting the cat under anesthesia and surgically amputating the claw tip and the last bone of the toe. Generally, only the front claws are removed, because the hind feet are not used for scratching furniture. While this procedure may offer a permanent solution to destructive clawing problems, it is not painless. After the operation, the cat suffers some pain and risk of infection as its mutilated paws heal.

There are other drawbacks, too. Because some of the major cat associations that sponsor cat shows do not allow declawed cats, the

procedure renders a cat ineligible for the show ring with these organizations. The procedure also inhibits climbing and self-defense, which means that cats allowed to roam freely outdoors should not be declawed and disadvantaged in this way. With only the front claws removed, a cat still can use its rear claws to climb trees, but it can't climb as well as before. Many people believe that robbing a cat of its natural defenses in this way may harm the animal psychologically and make it more apt to bite in self-defense. Some owners report profound personality changes in their cats after the surgery. Others say their cats developed inappropriate toilet habits afterward, probably as a result of cat box litter irritating the tender incisions. Older cats seem to have more difficulty adjusting to life without claws than kittens.

House-Soiling

Destructive clawing and house-soiling are the main reasons why many cats end up homeless in animal shelters. Sadly, some of these problem behaviors probably could have been easily prevented from the outset, if the owner had known what to expect and had been better prepared to deal with it.

Understanding what is normal behavior for cats under natural conditions is crucial to understanding how to deal with them when things go wrong under confined conditions. For example, cats, being naturally territorial, mark and defend areas where they spend most of their time. As discussed, clawing and spraying are two means of marking territory.

While spraying and litter box problems can occur in single-cat homes, they are more common in multicat households, particularly if you have too many cats crowded into too small an area. If you have more than one cat, you can help prevent elimination problems by providing each animal with its own litter box. Even then, the more aggressive cat may sometimes chase another away from the litter box. If this happens, place the boxes far enough apart to give each cat a sense of privacy and individual territory.

Generally, when a housebroken cat eliminates outside its litter box, it is either marking territory or displaying a preference for a particular spot, surface, or litter box filler. Cats do not begin house-soiling out of spite. At least, that's what the behavior experts say, although many owners can reel off accounts of cats urinating on shoes or other belongings of people who've irritated or neglected them. Such accounts are largely a matter of interpretation. Whatever the cause, house-soiling is often symptomatic of emotional anxiety or physical discomfort. Whenever a cat begins eliminating in inappropriate places, consider urinary tract infections and other medical causes first. If the cause turns out to be physical, prompt veterinary treatment can reverse the problem before it becomes an established habit. Always rule out disease or infection first, then pursue the behavioral or emotional approaches.

Spraying vs. Urinating

Determining whether a cat is spraying to mark territory or simply eliminating urine inappropriately can be difficult. Making the distinction, and understanding the difference, is important in deciding how to effectively treat a house-soiling problem. A few simple clues may help:

♦ If the urine stain appears to start primarily on a vertical surface—a wall or furniture leg—and drip down, then, the cat is spraying to mark territory.

♦ If the urine is pooled on a flat, horizontal surface—the floor or the bedcovers—the cat is squatting to eliminate urine.

Ascertaining this difference is crucial because the factors that motivate each type of behavior are different. To effectively deal with either undesirable behavior, you must try to eliminate the factors that appear to be causing or influencing the situation.

Here are some common motivating factors behind house-soiling problems:

Location preference: A cat that squats and inappropriately urinates on the carpet or floor may simply be expressing a dislike for the location of its litter box or for the texture of the

American Shorthair blue tabby adult.

litter. Perhaps the box is in a high foot-traffic area or too close to a noisy furnace that frightens the cat when operating. Try moving the box to a quieter, more secluded part of the house or, if possible, place it at or near the site of the house-soiling "accident."

Litter preference: If location doesn't seem to be a motivating factor, experiment with different types and textures of kitty litter. Some cats don't like their litter treated with fancy perfumes and deodorizers and will refuse to use them. Some cats prefer fine-grained litter that is like sand, while others are content with the larger, coarser clay granules.

Cleanliness: Often, failure to use the litter box occurs because cat and owner have different opinions as to what constitutes a clean litter box. Cats are fastidiously clean creatures, and digging in dirty, damp litter must be disgusting to them. If you're equally fastidious about removing the solid waste daily and replacing soiled litter weekly, your cat likely will be more happily inclined to use the box.

Anxiety: Emotional causes of house-soiling are even more difficult to pinpoint. Sometimes the sight of outdoor cats or the introduction of a new pet or a new baby into the household can trigger territorial spraying. In this situation, veterinarians can prescribe drugs that may ease the cat's anxiety and help suppress spraying and aggressive behaviors.

Whatever the cause, punishing a cat for spraying or eliminating in inappropriate places is seldom effective and often makes matters worse. Rather than resort to punishment, identify and change the behavior by trial-and-error removal of any possible motivating factors, one by one, until you hit upon the right one, and the problem resolves itself.

Cleaning up: To deter the cat from again using the same spot as a toilet, clean up accidents with enzymatic products that dissolve the odor. It is important to do this as quickly as possible, because the more times your cat uses the same place, the more ingrained the bad habit will become.

When cleaning up carpet stains, remember to clean the mat under the carpet, too, as the urine will have soaked through. Any traces of scent left will continue to attract the cat back to the same spot. If you can't lift the carpet to clean under it, use a syringe to inject solution under the rug, or soak the spot with an odor-neutralizing product. Several good odor-neutralizing products can be purchased at pet supply stores for cleaning up pet messes. A mix of white vinegar and warm water also works fairly well, but avoid ammonia-based cleaners. Ammonia is a urine by-product and might attract the cat back to the spot.

After you thoroughly clean and deodorize the spot, make the surface less appealing to the cat by covering it temporarily with plastic, aluminum foil, sandpaper, window screen, or double-sided tape. If possible, keep the cat completely away from the area for awhile to break the habit. For further reinforcement, use a water pistol or make a loud noise to startle the cat away from the area every time you see it near the spot. For a different approach, try changing the significance of the area by placing food and water bowls there. Cats typically will not eliminate where they eat.

The Feline Facts of Life

Because intact animals are much more likely to spray urine to mark territory or to express sexual status, you'll want to spay or neuter your American Shorthair to curb this undesirable tendency. It's still important to understand feline mating behavior to fully appreciate the species.

A breeding female cat is called a queen. An intact male is called a tom or stud. Ideally, a queen should not be bred until she is fully mature—at least one year old—although her first heat cycle (estrus) may occur months earlier. A tom reaches sexual maturity between 9 and 14 months, and from then on, his hormones drive him relentlessly to search for mates and to defend his territory against intruding toms. His sex hormones trigger his instinctive urge to spray and mark his territory with strong-smelling urine. A neutered male cat doesn't feel these urges and is less likely to spray.

Heat cycle: A queen comes into heat according to seasonal rhythms, usually in early spring, midsummer, and early fall. Feline reproductive cycles appear to be influenced by lengthening daylight hours, which explains why cats in the Northern Hemisphere cycle opposite to those in the southern half of the world. Most queens have heat cycles every two or three weeks during the breeding seasons; others cycle only once a month, but there are many exceptions.

Cat sex: When in season, an intact queen can be induced to assume the characteristic mating stance, called the estrus or lordotic posture, simply by gently stroking her back near the base of the tail. With front end pressed to the ground and with back hollowed, she will raise her hindquarters, swish her tail to one side, and tread up and down with her hind feet, as if marching in place. This is the position in which the tom mounts her from behind. The tom seizes her by the scruff of the neck and proceeds to pedal with his hind legs. The brief coupling generally ends with a howl and a hiss from the queen as the tom withdraws. She may even swing around to swat him with her paw.

Afterward, the two go off by themselves momentarily to groom or to eye one another from a short distance. Soon they will rejoin and repeat the mating sequence many more times. A free-roaming queen may mate with more than one male during her receptive stage and, as a result, deliver a mixed litter of kittens sired by different fathers.

Induced ovulation: Female cats are *induced ovulators*, meaning that the sex act must occur, usually repeatedly, to induce the release of eggs from the ovaries. To help accomplish this, the male's penis is ridged with tiny spines or barbs that scrape the inside of the queen's vagina during copulation. This physical stimulation apparently sends a message along nerve pathways to areas in the brain that release luteinizing hormone, a chemical that prompts ovulation.

Gestation and signs of pregnancy: If mating does not take place, the queen enters a stage of sexual inactivity until her next cycle begins; however, if the queen is bred and becomes pregnant, gestation normally lasts an average 65 or 66 days. About three weeks after conception, the queen's nipples redden, a condition described by breeders as pinking up. The queen's attitude may become more maternal and affectionate. Her appetite may increase, and she will gradually put on a few extra pounds. In about a month, her abdomen becomes noticeably swollen.

GROOMING YOUR AMERICAN SHORTHAIR

Fur serves to protect and insulate the cat from the elements. Generally speaking, a cat's coat consists of a topcoat of *guard* hairs over a soft undercoat of *down* and *awn* hairs. The coarser guard hairs protect the undercoat from the elements, the soft down hairs closest to the skin provide added warmth, while the awn hairs form a middle layer of insulation. The guard and awn hairs also can fluff out to trap air for better insulation.

One of the attractions of the American Shorthairs is that they do not require the daily grooming commitment that the long-haired breeds, such as the Persians and the Himalayans, demand. Nevertheless, their mink-like, dense, plush coats are not entirely mainte-nance-free. During the peak of shedding season, even shorthaired cats need a good combing every other day or so to remove the dead, loose hairs. Some regular attention to the coat during this time also means less hair left behind on your furniture, carpets, and clothes.

Regular grooming keeps your American Shorthair's coat clean and beautiful, reduces shedding, and helps prevent hair balls.

Shedding

While shedding may be more noticeable dur-ing the change of seasons—from winter to spring and from summer to fall—house cats liv-ing in artificial lighting tend to shed a little year-round. This is because the normal changes of hair coat aren't caused by seasonal tempera-ture changes, as one might assume; instead, experts say that environmental lighting governs the shedding process. Under natural conditions, the lengthening sunlight hours in early spring trigger the cat's body to shed hair and grow a new coat in preparation for the changing sea-son. Similarly, fall's shorter daylight hours cause the coat to thicken for winter. When artificial lighting extends the daylight hours in the cat's environment year-round, this natural cycle seems to get confused. The result is a coat that sheds slightly on a continual basis. Overheated homes in winter are also believed to play a role in making some house cats prone to shed more than normal, because the heat tends to dry the skin.

Benefits of Grooming

For the rest of the year, a weekly combing is sufficient to remove any loose, dead hair. Regu-lar combing is a healthful practice because it stimulates blood circulation in the skin and distributes natural oils through the coat, keeping it shiny and vibrant looking. It also helps prevent hair balls the inexpensive way. Fortunately, in shorthaired cats, these accumulations of hair in the stomach are not as frequent a nuisance as in longhaired cats, although the problem can occur.

By grooming your American Shorthair on a regular basis, you'll be much more likely to notice anything out of the ordinary—any concealed cuts, scratches, lumps, or bumps that may warrant veterinary investigation, for example, or even a hidden tick that has latched on for a blood meal.

You'll want to schedule a visit to the veterinarian if you ever notice that your American Shorthair's skin is looking dry or flaky, or if the coat appears dull, looks oily, smells bad, or feels brittle. Several medical and dietary problems can affect the skin and hair coat, including allergies, parasites, and hormonal or nutritional imbalances, among others.

First Steps in Grooming

Most cats love the attention they get during grooming and learn to tolerate their beauty sessions readily. If you take time to accustom your American Shorthair to the procedure early, starting at the kitten stage, and if you make each experience pleasurable, you will eventually be rewarded with a cat that looks forward to receiving your undivided attention during the sessions. With time and patience, the sessions can become an important human/feline bonding ritual.

To begin training your American Shorthair kitten, spend a few minutes each day gently combing the fur with a small, fine-toothed metal comb, taking special care not to rake the skin with the metal teeth. Keep the sessions short until the youngster gets used to being handled this way. Use the opportunity to get your American Shorthair accustomed to having its mouth gently opened, its ears touched, and its paws handled. This extra effort will pay off later when brushing teeth, administering medications, cleaning ears, and trimming claws.

Don't restrain your American Shorthair if its attention wanders elsewhere. Simply end the session and resume it again later. While grooming, hold the animal in your lap, or place it on a counter or table. Establish a regular grooming location and routine, and your kitten will quickly learn what's expected of it when you take it to that spot and pick up the comb. Maybe you like to have the cat rest in your lap while you groom and watch TV, or perhaps you prefer to stand and place the cat on a countertop or table. Regardless of where you choose to groom, be consistent about the place each time so your cat can learn from the repetition. Practice this routine daily for several weeks; once your American Shorthair accepts grooming graciously, gradually decrease the number of sessions to once or twice a week.

As your kitten grows, graduate to a medium-size metal comb. For convenience and versatility, some combs come with closely spaced teeth on one end and wider-spaced teeth on the other end. Use the fine-toothed end on the shorter hair around the face, head, and chin. Always end grooming sessions with a brief playtime, lots of praise, and maybe even a special treat, and your cat will eagerly anticipate the next one.

Combing and Brushing

When combing your American Shorthair, start at the base of the neck and gently comb the back and sides. Raise the chin a little to comb the throat and chest. When combing delicate areas, such as the belly, legs, and tail, be especially careful not to rake the comb's teeth against the cat's sensitive skin. Also, as you comb, remove any fur that may accumulate in the comb's teeth. Hair left in the comb tends to pull more hair out with it. If this pulling sensation becomes too heavy, your cat will experience discomfort. Any discomfort felt during the grooming session can cause the cat to associate pain and unpleasantness with the procedure, making it an unwilling candidate the next time. By all means, be extra gentle and avoid pulling the hair and skin.

During peak shedding periods, you may want to strip the coat occasionally by gently combing sections of fur against the way the hair lies. Called *back-combing*, this method removes the dead, loose hairs trapped closer to the skin as they are shed. To put the hair back in place, gently comb through it a second time, going in the direction the hair lies. If you intend to show your American Shorthair, you'll want to minimize stripping to keep the coat as full and plush as possible. Overstripping can make the coat look flat and thin. The majority of the time, simply comb *with* the lie of the hair, except when hair shedding is most noticeable.

If you notice any flea dirt in the coat, a fine-toothed metal comb makes a fine flea removal instrument, handily trapping the parasites and their excrement in the closely spaced teeth. To dispatch the fleas, simply dip the comb in a nearby pan of water until the insects have stopped moving and drowned. Then treat the flea problem appropriately (see pages 59–61 for information on controlling fleas).

Breeders' opinions differ widely on using brushes to groom cats. Because brush bristles can break the delicate hairs, some breeders recommend using them sparingly, if at all. If you try using a brush, and your cat seems to prefer it to a comb, choose a soft, natural-bristle brush for the task. This will help reduce breakage and static. Use the brush as you would the comb, brushing primarily *with* the lie of the fur.

Removing Mats

Fortunately, the American Shorthair's coat renders it relatively mat-free most of the time. Except for an occasional small mat in the "armpits" or on the belly, this particular grooming problem, more prevalent in longhaired breeds, seldom afflicts the short-coated cat. When matting does occur, however, it's important to remove the unsightly hair clump right away, no matter how small. The longer a mat remains in the coat, the tighter it pulls the skin, causing discomfort to the cat. If neglected too long, mats can irritate the skin severely enough to result in raw, open sores.

Inspect your cat's feet periodically for mats, too. Sometimes, tiny clumps of kitty litter or other debris can get stuck on the paw pads or between the toes and become especially painful. Mats in this area probably feel a lot like having a rock in your shoe.

Always remove any mats before bathing the cat, too, because water will set them permanently and make removal much more difficult. To remove a mat, separate the clump with your fingers and work it loose without yanking on the skin. To gently pick a stubborn mat loose, use the end teeth of a wide-toothed comb.

A dab of talcum powder, baby oil, or hair condi-tioner may help loosen a tight mat, but avoid using a greasy substance unless you're planning to bathe the cat afterward. As a last resort, use scissors or electric pet clippers to cut out stub-born mats, taking special care not to nick the skin. Your area pet supply store probably carries a selection of grooming clippers for dogs and cats, but with routine combing or brushing, you should not have to resort to using these expen-sive tools.

American Shorthair brown classic tabby. Matting is not a major grooming problem because of the Shorthair's coat length.

Trimming Claws

Besides grooming, toenail clipping is some-thing you should get your American Shorthair accustomed to at a young age. Like your finger-nails, cats' claws grow continuously and need to be clipped occasionally. Even with scratching

When trimming claws, clip only the white tips. Avoid cutting into the pink quick, as this will cause pain and bleeding.

posts available, an indoor cat's nails do not wear down as readily as those of an outdoor cat. Neglected, untrimmed claws can curve under and grow back into the paw pads, causing a painful swelling and abscess. Trim claws once a month or so and always prior to a cat show, if you intend to exhibit. Regular trimming reduces the risk of injury to yourself and other family members and helps prevent snags in your carpets and furnishings.

Cats retract their claws when not in use. To extend them for trimming, hold the paw with your thumb on top and fingers on the bottom and gently squeeze. Before clipping, look closely at the nail and identify the *quick.* If the nail is white, the quick clearly shows up as a thin pink line running about three-fourths of the way down the nail toward the tip. To avoid cutting into the sensitive quick, trim the nail tip below the pink line. The quick contains nerves and blood vessels, but the nail tip below it does not. If you accidentally cut too high up into the pink quick, the cat will feel pain and the nail will bleed. If this happens, hold pressure over the wound with a cotton ball until the blood clots, or apply a shaving styptic.

With the cat held securely in your lap or placed on the countertop or table with a towel over it to prevent the cat from slipping, trim the claws on the front and hind feet. Start by

clipping just two or three nails at a time, then add more as your American Shorthair gets accustomed to the idea. Use human or pet nail clippers for the job, then smooth the rough edges with an emery board or nail file. Don't forget the fifth claw slightly higher up on each inside forepaw.

Although they have short coats, these cats still benefit from regular grooming.

If you are going to show your American Shorthair, it will require a bath a day or two before the show to look its best in the ring; otherwise, bathing your American Shorthair becomes necessary only if the coat becomes flea-infested, excessively oily, or otherwise soiled. Too many baths can rob your American Shorthair's coat of natural oils and dry the skin, so bathe only when your cat truly needs it.

Intact toms seem particularly prone to developing an oily condition called stud tail, which requires more frequent bathing to keep under control. Characterized by a waxy, brown buildup at the base and top ridge of the tail, this unsightly condition is caused by overactive glands. If not periodically cleansed, the greasy accumula-

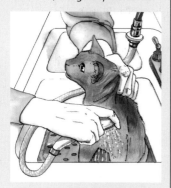

When bathing your cat, use warm water, not hot. If you use a spray nozzle, keep the water pressure low and never spray the water directly in the cat's face.

Assemble the supplies you need before you start to bathe your cat.

tion can form a crust on the skin and infect the hair follicles, causing sores and hair loss on the tail. Neutering the male cat usually eliminates this unpleasant condition.

Things You'll Need

Every breeder and exhibitor has special preferences when it comes to shampoos and such, so start with what your breeder recommends. Use only products labeled as *Safe for Cats. Never* use dog shampoos or dog flea products on a cat, because the medication or flea insecticide in canine preparations may be too strong, even fatal, for cats. Also, not all cat flea products are safe for use on kittens, so read labels carefully before applying any shampoo, spray, dip, or powder to a kitten's fur. If the label doesn't specifically say that the product is safe for use on kittens, don't risk using it.

Start getting your kitten used to baths after age four months, but don't overdo it.

In addition to shampoo, other supplies you'll need for the bath include:

- a comb
- cotton balls (for swabbing the ears)
- a blow dryer
- towels
- a washcloth
- a sink or tub
- a pitcher or shower spray attachment
- a source of clean, warm water for washing and rinsing

The kitchen sink is usually the ideal place for the job, but if you must bathe the cat in a laundry tub, reserve a second tub of clean water for rinsing. For blow-drying the cat, you'll need a table or countertop with access to an electrical outlet. You'll probably also need a willing assistant, because many cat baths easily turn into two-person productions, especially if the feline is not fond of or used to the idea.

Before You Start

To minimize the risk of injury to you and your assistant, trim the cat's claws first. Also before bathing, give the coat a thorough combing to remove mats or loose, dead hairs that could get tangled or set in wet fur.

If possible, close off the room where the bath will take place, so you won't have to chase a wet, soapy escapee through the house. Before putting the cat in the tub or sink, fill the basin partially with warm (not hot) water. A rubber bath mat in the bottom prevents slipping and makes the cat feel more secure by giving it something to grip.

How to Bathe

Have your assistant hold the cat down in the partially filled water basin with gentle pressure on the back and shoulders. If the cat panics, talk to it reassuringly and gently hold it down by the scruff of the neck until it stops struggling. Be careful not to splash water in the cat's face or dunk its head under, as this will only increase its panic and create havoc for you and your assistant.

Wet the fur first with warm water, using the pitcher to dip and pour over the cat's back. If using a spray nozzle, keep the water pressure low to avoid frightening the cat. Don't spray water directly in the face. After wetting the fur sufficiently, apply shampoo and form a lather, starting at the neck and working back toward the tail. To lather the belly, have your assistant hold up the front legs. Avoid getting soap near the face and eyes. Use a damp washcloth or moistened cotton balls to gently wet the head and wipe the face and eye areas clean.

How to Rinse

To remove all traces of shampoo, spend twice as much time rinsing as you do lathering. Any residue left behind could make the coat look flat and greasy and cause itching and irritation. Use the spray nozzle to rinse, or put the cat in a tub of clean, warm water, then dip and pour the water from the pitcher. When the fur feels squeaky clean, drain off the water and gently press out the excess by running your hands down the back, legs, and tail. Lift the cat out of

Before blow drying your cat, wrap it in a towel and dry the wet fur as much as possible.

the tub or sink, being careful to support its rear end with one hand, and place it on a table or countertop for drying.

How to Blow Dry

First, towel dry the sopping fur as much as possible, but towel drying alone simply can't remove all of the moisture. Finishing with the blow dryer is necessary to prevent the cat from chilling. Like bathing, many cats learn to tolerate blow drying if you exercise some sensitivity when introducing them to the idea. Use only the low settings, never the hottest one—and never blow air directly in the cat's face.

Gently comb the fur as you blow dry, or separate the damp hair with your fingers, starting at the neck and working back toward the tail. Don't forget to dry the underside. Have your assistant hold up the front legs for easier access to the belly and between the hind legs.

Don't Forget to Clean the Ears

Finally, use cotton balls to gently wipe away any dirt or wax visible just inside the ear flaps. Never poke cotton swabs or other objects into the ear canal, as this could cause injury to the delicate inner ear structures. If the ears show an excessive amount of dirty, crumbly, brown wax inside, or if they exude a fruity odor, have your veterinarian check for ear mites or fungal infections.

SHOWING YOUR AMERICAN SHORTHAIR

Cat Show Organization

Cat shows originated in Great Britain. In the United States, cat exhibits and judgings have taken place since the 1870s, but the first official all-breed show was held in 1895. The Cat Fanciers' Association (CFA), incorporated in 1919, is the world's largest registry of pedigree cats, sponsoring about 400 shows a year across the United States and internationally through its more than 650 member clubs.

In the United States, judging takes place on *judging tables* set up in one area of the show hall in full view of all spectators and exhibitors attending. Behind each judging table is a row of cages, where cats entered in the same category are called to await judging. This setup of tables and cages is called a *judging ring*.

A single exhibition may have four or more judging rings set up, each operating as a separate competition and presided over by a different judge. Sometimes, separate clubs present back-to-back shows consisting of eight to ten rings over a two-day weekend. Cats can compete in all rings for which they are eligible. In the ring, the judge removes each cat from its cage, places it on the judging table in view of the audience, and

Visiting cat shows is a good way to learn more about cats and cat care.

thoroughly examines it. After evaluating all cats in the ring, the judge awards at least first-, second- and third-place ribbons to the winners. All pedigreed cats are judged according to how closely they meet the written standard of perfection for their particular breed, pattern, and color.

All-breed and specialty shows: If the show is an *all-breed* show, all cats, regardless of their type, compete against each other. *Specialty* shows, on the other hand, may be restricted to longhaired or shorthaired breeds, among other specialties. Depending on the association sponsoring the show, various divisions and classes exist for eligible pedigreed cats, altered cats, kittens, household pets, and new or experimental breeds and colors. Generally, unaltered, adult pedigreed cats begin their show careers competing in *open* classes against others of their breed, sex, and color. After achieving a specified number of wins, they become a champion and can compete against other champions for the coveted title of grand champion. Many associations award additional titles beyond these.

Alter classes, called *premiership* in the CFA, allow spayed and neutered pedigreed cats to compete against other altered cats of the same breed. Altered cats are judged according to the same standards as whole or intact cats, but instead of qualifying as a champion or grand champion, they earn comparable titles of premier or grand premier in the CFA. Many novice exhibitors prefer to show in alter classes. If you want to show your American Shorthair, but you have no interest in breeding it, showing in premier or alter classes may be the best route to go.

Pedigreed kittens between four and eight (or in some associations, ten) months old can compete in classes with other kittens of their breed. The household pet (HHP) competition is for mixed-breed or nonpedigreed cats, which must be spayed or neutered. Policies vary, but some associations permit a purebred cat to be shown as a household pet, as long as the owner surrenders the papers or does not register the cat as a purebred. Household pets are judged for their beauty, personality, and overall condition, rather than against a formal breed standard.

New Breeds and Colors

Most shows allow experimental breeds and colors of cats to be exhibited in nonchampionship classes, which generally are called Provisional, Miscellaneous, or New Breeds and Colors (NBC). Practices for accepting and showing new breeds, colors, and varieties differ among the associations. In general, experimental breeds are exhibited first in noncompetitive, miscellaneous, NBC, or AOV (Any Other Variety) classes before being granted prechampionship, or provisional breed, status. Cats in provisional breed competition are judged according to a provisional standard, but once their new breed gains full recognition, they become eligible for championship classes.

Breed Standard

Every cat competing in a show is judged according to how well it meets the standard for its particular breed. A breed standard is a written blueprint describing the ideal conformation and coloring of animals representing that breed.

From time to time, the breed standard may be revised or rewritten by formal committees that convene periodically to amend and update them. This is because selective breeding sometimes results in new colors or varieties that may be added to the standard after meeting certain criteria for acceptance. The breed standard can also vary among the different cat associations, as well as from country to country. Practices for accepting new colors and varieties vary widely, too, and some associations or countries may recognize colors not currently accepted elsewhere. Addresses and Web sites for the North American cat registries are listed in the back of this book.

Showing Your Cat

Showing is a fun and worthwhile way to learn a lot about all types of cats. A good way to become involved in showing cats is to join a cat club in your area that is affiliated with one of the cat-registering associations (see page 92). For club information and show rules, call or write the association(s) in which your cat is registered. Some registries charge a small fee to cover the cost of printing and mailing their rule booklets. The breeder of your cat should also be willing to help you get started, because your wins in the show ring will reflect favorably on his or her bloodlines and cattery name.

If you're not involved with a club, check cat magazine show date listings, then write or call the number given for entry forms and information. Complete the entry form by the specified deadline and return it to the entry clerk along with the appropriate fee. You also may request

to be *benched* next to your breeder or to someone you know who is an experienced exhibitor.
Your "benching assignment" is the cage where
your cat will stay when it's not being judged in
one of the rings.

Show Supplies

Generally, the show committee provides
a chair at each cage, cat litter, and sometimes
disposable litter boxes. You'll have to bring a
small litter box, just in case, plus your grooming
equipment, a grooming table (a sturdy TV tray
or plastic patio table serve the same purpose),
a cat carrier, a cat bed, food and water bowls,
your cat's favorite food, fabric or towels to line
the sides and bottom of the cage, and any other
accessories to make your cat feel comfortable.
Of course, you will have completed most of your
American Shorthair's grooming at home, having
bathed it a day or two before the show. Only
touch-ups should be required at the show.

The Day of the Show

After you check in at the door on the day of
the show and get your cat settled in its assigned
cage, read the catalog schedule to determine
when your cat will be judged. Listen to the public address system, and when you hear your cat's
number called, carry your cat to the appropriate
judging ring. Your number will be posted on top
of one of the cages in the ring. Place your cat in
the correct cage, then take a seat to watch.

Judging

The judge will examine each cat in turn on
the table and hang ribbons on the winners'
cages at the end of the class. When the judging
is over, the clerk will ask the exhibitors to
remove their cats from the ring.

Depending on how well your cat does, it may
be called back for finals, when the top contes-
tants in a given category are presented. The
highest awards at a show include Best of
Breed and the most coveted prize, Best in
Show. Cats that win in the championship or
premiership finals earn points based on the
number of cats defeated at the show. These
points count toward regional and national titles.
To understand the ribbons, points, and awards
system more fully, consult the rules booklet prepared by the cat fancy association sponsoring
the show.

An Owner's Responsibility

Whether you're on the road with your
American Shorthair enroute to a cat show
or arranging for its care while you're away,
remember that your conscientiousness as a
cat owner will inevitably be noticed by others.
In this way, you have an opportunity to demonstrate to others how to properly tend to a
feline companion. Many cat owners take this
responsibility seriously and strive to become
the best-educated pet owners they can be.
They visit shows, attend pet care seminars,
participate in clubs, and read books and
magazines about cats.

Such an attitude is admirable because the
American Shorthair kitten you acquire and
raise to adulthood represents a significant
financial and emotional investment on your
part, as well as on the part of your breeder.
The more strongly you communicate the value
of this investment to others, the more likely you
are to instill a similar appreciation in others
regarding your chosen breed, and about cats
in general.

INFORMATION

North American Cat Registries

American Association of Cat
Enthusiasts (AACE)
P.O. Box 213
Pine Brook, NJ 07058
(973) 335-6717
Web page: http://www.
aaceinc.org

American Cat Association (ACA)
8101 Katherine Avenue
Panorama City, CA 91402
(818) 781-5656

American Cat Fanciers
Association (ACFA)
P.O. Box 203
Point Lookout, MO 65726
(417) 334-5430
Web page: http://www.
acfacat.com

Canadian Cat Association (CCA)
220 Advance Boulevard
Suite 101
Brampton, Ontario
Canada L6T 4J5
(905) 459-1481
Web page: http://www.
cca-afc.com

Cat Fanciers' Association (CFA)
1805 Atlantic Avenue
P.O. Box 1005
Manasquan, NJ 08736-0805
(732) 528-9797
Web page: http://www.cfainc.org

Cat Fanciers' Federation (CFF)
Box 661
Gratis, OH 45330
(937) 787-9009
Web page: http://www.cffinc.org

National Cat Fanciers'
Association (NCFA)
10215 West Mount Morris Road
Flushing, MI 48433
(810) 659-9517

The International Cat
Association (TICA)
P.O. Box 2684
Harlingen, TX 78551
(956) 428-8046
Web page: http://www.covesoft.
com/tca/

United Feline Organization (UFO)
P.O. Box 3234
Lacey, WA 98509-3234
(360) 438-6903
Web page: http://ufo1nw@aol.com

Important Organizations

American Society for the
Prevention of Cruelty to
Animals (ASPCA)
424 East 92nd Street
New York, NY 10128-6804

Association of American Feed
Control Officials, Inc. (AAFCO)
c/o Georgia Department of
Agriculture
Agriculture Building, Capitol Square
Atlanta, GA 30334

Cornell Feline Health Center
Cornell University College of
Veterinary Medicine
Ithaca, NY 14853
(607) 253-3414

The Delta Society
P.O. Box 1080
Renton, WA 98057
(425) 226-7357

Food and Drug Administration's
Center for Veterinary Medicine
(FDA-CVM)
7500 Standish Place
Rockville, MD 20855

The Humane Society of the United
States (HSUS)
2100 L Street, NW
Washington, DC 20037
(202) 452-1100

National Animal Poison
Control Center
University of Illinois College of
Veterinary Medicine
2001 South Lincoln Avenue
Urbana, IL 61801
(800) 548-2423
(900) 680-0000
Note: Fee charged for crisis
management

Cat Publications

CATS Magazine
Subscriptions:
P.O. Box 56886
Boulder, CO 80322-6886
(800) 829-9125

Corporate offices:
2 News Plaza
P.O. Box 1790
Peoria, IL 61656
(209) 682-6626

Cat Fancy
Subscriptions:
P.O. Box 52864
Boulder, CO 80322-2864
(800) 365-4421

Editorial offices:
P.O. Box 6050
Mission Viejo, CA 92690
(949) 855-8822

Cat Fancier's Almanac
Cat Fanciers' Association
1805 Atlantic Avenue
P.O. Box 1005
Manasquan, NJ 08736-0805
(732) 528-9797

CATsumer Report
P.O. Box 10069
Austin, TX 78766-1069
(800) 968-1738

Catnip (newsletter)
Tufts University School of
 Veterinary Medicine
Subscriptions:
P.O. Box 420235
Palm Coast, FL 32142
(800) 829-0926

CatWatch (newsletter)
Cornell University College of
 Veterinary Medicine
Subscriptions:
P.O. Box 420235
Palm Coast, FL 32142
(800) 829-8893

Books

Behrend, Katrin and Wegler,
 Monika. The Complete Book of
 Cat Care. Hauppauge, New York:
 Barron's Educational Series, Inc.,
 1991.
Carlson, Delbert G., D.V.M., and Gif-
 fin, James M., M.D. Cat Owner's
 Veterinary Handbook. New York,
 New York: Howell Book House,
 1983.
Davis, Karen Leigh. Fat Cat, Finicky
 Cat: A Pet Owner's Guide to
 Pet Food and Feline Nutrition.
 Hauppauge, New York: Barron's
 Educational Series, Inc., 1997.
____. Somali Cats: A Complete Pet
 Owner's Manual. Hauppauge,
 New York: Barron's Educational
 Series, Inc., 1996.
____. The Exotic Shorthair Cat: A
 Complete Pet Owner's Manual.
 Hauppauge, New York: Barron's
 Educational Series, Inc., 1997.
____. Turkish Angora Cats: A
 Complete Pet Owner's Manual.
 Hauppauge, New York: Barron's
 Educational Series, Inc., 1998.
Helgren, J. Anne. Encyclopedia of
 Cat Breeds: A Complete Guide to
 the Domestic Cats of North
 America. Hauppauge, New York:
 Barron's Educational Series, Inc.,
 1997.
Robinson, Roy. Genetics for Cat
 Breeders. 3rd ed. Oxford: Perga-
 mon Press, 1991.
Siegal, Mordecai and Cornell Uni-
 versity. The Cornell Book of Cats.
 New York, New York: Villard
 Books, 1989.
Taylor, David. The Ultimate Cat
 Book. New York, New York:
 Simon and Schuster, 1989.
____. You and Your Cat: A Complete
 Guide to the Health, Care &
 Behavior of Cats. New York, New
 York: Alfred A. Knopf, 1986.
Whiteley, H. Ellen, D.V.M. Under-
 standing and Training Your Cat or
 Kitten. New York, New York:
 Crown Trade Paperbacks, 1994.
Wright, Michael and Walters, Sally,
 eds. The Book of the Cat. New
 York, New York: Summit Books,
 1980.

Photo Credits

Chanan Photography: pages 2–3,
8, 13, 16, 28, 33, 41, 53, 56, 57, 60,
64, 72, 73, 77, 80, 84, 85, 88, 93; Larry
Johnson: page 4; Bonnie Nance:
pages 12, 17, 20, 24, 25, 29, 32, 36,
40, 44, 45, 52, 68.

Cover Photos

Chanan Photography: front cover,
back cover; Norvia Behling: inside
front cover, inside back cover.

Calico American Shorthair. A calico is basically a white cat, usually female, with mingling patches of black and red.

About the Author

Karen Leigh Davis, a professional member of the Cat Writers' Association, has a background in journalism and business writing. She has written a pet care column and numerous feature articles on cats and other companion animals for national and regional magazines and newspapers. As a freelance writer with more than 15 years of experience, she has conducted extensive research on animal-related topics with veterinarians, breeders, and other experts. Davis comes from a cat-loving family and has a lifetime of experience living in the company of cats. She has bred and shown Persians and Himalayans, but she finds all felines, purebred or mixed, domestic or wild, irresistibly charming and beautiful. She lives in Roanoke, Virginia, with four Persian cats.

Other Barron's titles by Karen Leigh Davis:
Somali Cats (1996)
The Exotic Shorthair Cat (1997)
Fat Cat, Finicky Cat (1997)
Turkish Angora Cats (1998)

Important Note

When you handle cats, you may sometimes get scratched or bitten. If this happens, have a doctor treat the injuries immediately.

Make sure your cat receives all the necessary shots and dewormings, otherwise serious danger to the animal and to human health may arise. A few diseases and parasites can be communicated to humans. If your cat shows any signs of illness, you should definitely consult a veterinarian. If you are worried about your own health, see your doctor and tell him or her that you have cats.

Some people have allergic reactions to cats. If you think you might be allergic, see your doctor before you get a cat.

It is possible for a cat to cause damage to someone else's property and even to cause accidents. For your own protection you should make sure your insurance covers such eventualities, and you should definitely have liability insurance.

All inquiries should be addressed to:
Barron's Educational Series, Inc.
250 Wireless Boulevard
Hauppauge, New York 11788

http://www.barronseduc.com

International Standard Book No. 0-7641-0658-9

Library of Congress Catalog Card No. 98-44057

Library of Congress Cataloging-in-Publication Data
Davis, Karen Leigh, 1953–
    American shorthair cats : everything about purchase, care, nutrition, health care, behavior, and showing / Karen Leigh Davis : illustrations by Michele Earle-Bridges.
        p.   cm. — (A complete pet owner's manual)
    Includes bibliographical references (p. 92) and index.
    ISBN 0-7641-0658-9 (pbk.)
    1. American shorthair cat.   I. Title.   II. Series.
SF449.A45D38   1999
636.8'22—dc21   98-44057
                                                        CIP

Printed in Hong Kong

9 8 7 6 5 4 3 2 1

American Shorthairs consistently rank in the top ten most popular breeds of cat and are considered one of the most beloved pets in the United States. They have an easygoing temperament and are playful animals with instinctual intelligence. American Shorthairs thrive on human companionship and develop devoted attachments to their owners.